How to Add
MEDICAL WEIGHT LOSS
—TO—
YOUR PRACTICE

7 Steps to an Enjoyable Business, Healthier Patients and Increased Profitability

KAROL H. CLARK

5 – Time #1 Best-Selling Author

For additional Free resources and training, go to www.WeightLossPracticeBuilder.com

DEDICATION

This book is dedicated to all of the physicians who have trained tirelessly and devoted their careers to diagnosing and treating the many diseases and ailments that plague their patients. It is dedicated to physicians that want to enjoy the practice of medicine again rather than living on the brink of burn out due to increased rules/regulations, low reimbursement and the demand to focus more on volume and less on what you love - true 'patient care'.

This book is also dedicated to my hard working, visionary husband Tom, who is one of the most intelligent and patient people I know. You help transform lives through significant surgical and medical weight loss with integrity, honesty and a true love for those you serve. You are a terrific husband, best friend and dad.

Thank you to our wonderful staff who happily give their time and share their talents with those we serve each and every day. Your enthusiasm, care and loyalty are second to none!

CONTENTS

About This Book vii

Introduction 1

CHAPTER 1:   Top Trends in Medical Weight Loss 3

CHAPTER 2:   Risks/Benefits of Adding Medical
Weight Loss to Your Practice 17

CHAPTER 3:   YOUR Big Advantage 23

CHAPTER 4:   Step 1 – Do Your Research & Create
YOUR Vision 25

CHAPTER 5:   Step 2 – Determine Your Business
Model & Key Program Components 31

CHAPTER 6:   Step 3 – Identify Your Resources/Join
Obesity Medicine Association 57

CHAPTER 7:   Step 4 – Surround Yourself with
Great People, Train them and Treat
them Well 59

CHAPTER 8:   Step 5 – Create Your Business Plan
and Budget 65

CHAPTER 9:   Step 6 – Add Retail/Build Systems 69

CHAPTER 10: Step 7 – GREAT Process to Market, Measure ROI and Grow Your Practice.... 83

CHAPTER 11: The Simplest, Most Cost Effective Way to Get Started 105

Bonus Chapters (Adapted in part from the #1 Best-Selling Book 5 *Profit Engines of a Successful Bariatric Surgery Practice*): 111

CHAPTER 12: Social Media that Supports Your Practice and Your Patients 113

CHAPTER 13: Keys to Effective Practice Management 121

About the Author 131

References 133

ABOUT THIS BOOK

This book is a business guide on how to build, promote and grow a successful medical weight loss practice based upon decades of weight loss practice management. This book was written for any physician who is interested in adding medical weight loss to their practice. Most commonly, this includes primary care physicians and bariatric surgeons, whether independent or based within a hospital setting or medical group.

This book is not a guide for clinical pathways or prescriptive medicine. Such information is ever-changing and best provided by your professional organizations and through your experience/training. I strongly recommend you join the Obesity Medicine Association and consider board certification through the American Board of Obesity Medicine.

I realize that time is your greatest asset and something that is extremely limited. I tried to keep this book short enough to give you what you need and yet provide the necessary information if you want to dive deeper into the business and marketing of your successful medical weight loss practice. The information is intended to provide you with new ideas and specific implementation guidelines so you can shorten your learning curve.

This results in quicker implementation and greater profitability for your business.

If you are short on time, I recommend you focus on the 7 steps along with chapter 11 which outlines the easiest path to get your profitable medical weight loss program up and running quickly.

The bonus chapters were included due to the overwhelmingly positive feedback I received regarding the content from one of my prior best-selling books, *5 Profit Engines of a Successful Bariatric Surgery Practice.* The information has been updated and is applicable to medical weight loss as well.

I am not just a theoretical consultant. I am in the trenches of running a profitable 10,000 square foot comprehensive weight loss facility in Virginia (www.cfwls.com). I also actively consult with various practices and corporations throughout the United States. I can relate firsthand to the unique needs of bariatric surgeons (I am married to one), primary care physicians and the patients they serve. I fully understand the need for profitability, efficient systems, improved long-term patient outcomes and overall enjoyment for all involved. I not only understand these needs, I actively work with our team to make these outcomes a reality each day.

Bottom line, your success is my goal. I am ALWAYS committed to a positive return on investment (ROI) whether you just read this book, license use of one of our turn-key weight loss programs or invest in individualized consultation services.

Sometimes people purchase a book such as this and read it for the information and get excited about implementation and then...do nothing. I implore you to take action. Remember, one person cannot do it all. Share this information with your team and develop your action plan together. If you feel stuck, don't hesitate to schedule a 30 minute free strategy session with me. I can be reached at Karol@WeightLossPracticeBuilder.com or you can schedule with me directly at www.smarturl.it/bookkarol.

I am also interested in your feedback and connecting with you. Please connect with me on LinkedIn at www.linkedin.com/in/clarkkarol. You can also find many free tips and actionable information via my blog and podcast – *Build the Weight Loss Practice of Your Dreams* at www.WeightLossPracticeBuilder.com. *Let me know if you would like to be a guest on my podcast as well. I love interviewing physicians who are making a positive difference in the world!*

INTRODUCTION

There are a number of emotions that can go hand in hand with creating a weight loss practice or any new venture. Such emotions occur whether you are self-employed or employed by a larger health system. These emotions range from excitement, pride, confidence, appreciation and enjoyment to fear, exhaustion, frustration, burn out and depression. It is my mission to help physicians, administrators and support staff to build profitable weight loss programs so they worry less, achieve more, *have outstanding patient outcomes* and enjoy the process along the way.

Weight Loss Practice Builder, my books and turn-key weight loss programs came about because I was approached by various primary care physicians, bariatric surgeons, bariatricians, health systems, medical corporations and nutritional corporations regarding the comprehensive weight loss business that my husband and I have built and operate in Newport News, Virginia. It was the first of its kind in the region over a decade ago combining surgical weight loss, medical weight loss, fitness, onsite and online education along with a robust retail nutritional store. They wanted to know if it was a 'chain' or if we had thought of franchising. Franchising is not particularly something we are interested in doing at this time. However, I knew I was interested in working one on one with such individuals so they could duplicate our success, help more patients and experience more enjoyment in their business. I hope this book helps you do the same!

Whether you are building a weight loss practice from the ground up or striving to grow your existing program, you are about to learn a formula that will help you meet or exceed industry standards and ensure the long term viability of your program. All while improving patient outcomes, enhancing your bottom line and resulting in more enjoyment and satisfaction for you, your partners, your employees and your patients. So let's get started!

1

TOP TRENDS IN MEDICAL WEIGHT LOSS

B efore we get to the specifics of how to build, manage and market your successful medical weight loss program, it's important to briefly review obesity as it is understood today along with some documented trends and intuitive personal predictions. Staying ahead of the curve to best serve your patients (and be ahead of your competition) depends upon understanding trends of what the future may hold so you can prepare adequately and set into action a proactive plan.

As you know, obesity was officially recognized as a disease by the American Medical Association in 2013.[1] Although some still debate this designation, the reality remains that there is more to being overweight than a lack of willpower and genetics. This disease and its many related co-morbid conditions necessitate treatment by trained healthcare professionals able to educate and engage patients in lasting behavior modification.

This designation helped to open the door to additional research, coordination of care and improved resources. However, this designation does not negate the fact that weight loss requires much work and dedication. Patients must integrate healthier habits into their everyday life in order to ensure short and long term weight loss results. This is an important tenet to understand and an integral message for every weight loss program to impart to their weight loss patients who are often simply seeking a 'quick fix'.

Below are a few statistics that, while alarming, will likely not surprise you since you see this every day in your practice.[2]

1. In the United States, 36.5% of the population are obese (BMI >30) and an additional 32.5% of Americans are overweight (BMI 25-29.9).
2. Obesity affects 12.7 million American children (1 in 6).
3. Obesity is linked to more than 60 chronic diseases.
4. Obesity treatment costs Americans $147 billion each year.
5. As of 2017, all 50 states have an obesity rate over 20%. Just 2 decades ago, no state had an obesity rate over 15%.

So, with 2/3 of the American population designated as overweight, it is no surprise that weight loss is one of the TOP goals for most people. They desire weight loss so much in fact, that it is estimated that the U.S. weight loss market was worth $68.2 billion in 2017 which is a 2.7% gain from the previous year and is expected to rise about 3.2% to $70 billion in 2018.[3]

Great news! Or is it? It is obviously *not* great news that obesity is an epidemic, but is it great news that people are spending $70 billion per year for treatment?

As with every 'hot' industry, spending brings quality solutions. However, it also brings out droves of people and corporations looking to make a buck from desperate people with an identified need when they may not necessarily have a great service or product that helps the underlying problem. They also may not have the knowledge to offer proper and safe treatment either.

Unfortunately, while spending is up, people don't always want to pay for what physicians have to offer. Rather, they would prefer to spend money on quick fix gimmicks and medications that often just mask the underlying problem(s) and seek healthcare advice for *free*. As a result, offering quality medically supervised weight loss services, just like many facets of healthcare, can be frustrating to say the least.

> *Unfortunately, while spending is up,*
> *people don't always want to pay for what*
> *physicians have to offer.*

I propose that this is all the more reason to offer a medical weight loss program as long as you are committed to the highest quality of services, education, patient engagement, long-term results and ongoing support. Patients don't need a band aid, they need to be guided and monitored (often with tough love), especially those with co-morbid conditions that are affected by weight and require close monitoring. Your patients respect you and you may be one of the most influential people that can get through to them to change their habits for good. In addition, with effective services and marketing, physicians can grow their

KAROL H. CLARK

practice and their profits by offering medical weight loss services. This can create significant positive life changing results. This is where the fun comes in!

Your patients respect you and you may be one of the most influential people that can get through to them to change their habits for good.

So let's take a look at my predicted trends for medical weight loss over the next 5 years based upon research as well as a bit of intuition.

Karol's Top Trends in Medical Weight Loss

Trend #1	There will be an increase in medically supervised weight loss programs being integrated into primary care offices and bariatric surgery offices
Trend #2	New research based treatment modalities for medically supervised weight loss programs will continue to evolve
Trend #3	Professional obesity medicine membership will continue to increase along with board certification
Trend #4	Commercial, retail weight loss programs and multi-level weight loss marketers will continue to grow in numbers and capture a large part of the population seeking quick weight loss solutions
Trend #5	There will be continued dwindling of physician insurance reimbursement & higher premiums for patients
Trend #6	There will be an increase in concierge cash pay medically supervised weight loss programs (with the Proper Mindset & Marketing Plan)
Trend #7	Medical weight loss practices will have a need for additional practice revenue streams
Trend #8	Patient expectations will continue to rise when paying for concierge medical weight loss
Trend #9	There will be an increased focus on clean eating and environmental friendly options for patients

303

Trend #1: There will be an increase in medically supervised weight loss programs being integrated into primary care offices and bariatric surgery offices.

At the risk of sounding old, my husband and I remember going to national conferences for weight loss surgery and medical weight loss with just about 200 participants. At the time of this publication, conferences such as Obesity Week now attracts over 4,000 professional each year and the number continues to increase. This particular conference is sponsored jointly by The Obesity Society (TOS) and the American Society for Metabolic and Bariatric Surgery (ASMBS) and attracts participants both from within the United States and across the globe internationally.

At these conferences, I have found that an incredible number of physicians from various specialties are looking to integrate medical weight loss into their practice or open a new cash pay medical weight loss practice to escape their current reality. I have literally spent hours listening to their stories and talking to them about options, considerations and program design. It is my hope that those that follow through will experience success and do so with a quality program that makes a difference in the lives of the millions of people who need such services.

Trend #2: New research based treatment modalities for medically supervised weight loss programs will continue to evolve.

Weight loss is fascinating and ever changing. As with any field of medicine, practitioners need to stay abreast of the latest research and integrate new treatment modalities as they see fit. In addition, with weight loss, I feel practitioners need to 'practice what they preach' so they are a good example to those they serve.

At our practice, it is an expectation and a 'perk' for staff to be able to participate in all facets of our weight loss programs (nutritional products, counseling, fitness classes, educational classes, online programs and the like). If someone is bringing in a lunch, we have specific requests to not include pasta, bread, sweets and the like. In addition, we all pitch in to provide recipes, create fun events, record podcasts, implement entertaining contests, host webinars and offer support groups (online and onsite) to keep our patients engaged. We truly try to live what we teach... without losing sight of enjoying life.

As new treatment modalities are explored such as intermittent fasting, our physician actually tries it (usually along with me as his wife) and he livestreams his daily progress and/or the experiences of those willing to share. You have to make it fun! Our entire staff taste tests new products and nothing is introduced that isn't 'blessed' by the physician and staff. Coincidentally, that makes it easier for them to sell products and services which is an added bonus!

Trend #3: Professional obesity medicine membership will continue to increase along with board certifications.

This trend is likely no surprise. With more practitioners jumping on the medical weight loss band wagon, they will want to reach out to professional organizations for the latest information. They will also seek board certification for additional expertise and recognition. This is a good thing.

A primary resource is the Obesity Medicine Association. They are the largest organization of physicians, nurse practitioners, physician assistants and other health care providers working every day to improve the lives of patients affected by obesity.[4]

For physicians seeking certification, the American Board of Obesity Medicine (ABOM) is the official entity certifying physicians in the treatment of obesity. Physicians who complete the ABOM certification process in obesity medicine are designated Diplomates of the American Board of Obesity Medicine.[5]

Trend #4: Commercial, retail weight loss programs and multi-level weight loss marketers will continue to grow in numbers and capture a large part of the population seeking quick weight loss solutions

Let's face it, everywhere you look, the next best weight loss and diet plan is being advertised. Jenny Craig®, Weight Watchers®, NutriSystem®, South Beach Diet™, vitamin stores, pharmacies and many individual coaches/solopreneurs to name a few. In fact, for the commercial diets, market analysts are expecting a 12.7% gain to $3.55 billion in business for 2018.[3]

While I prefer professional services for weight loss, as far as I am concerned, whatever WORKS for a person is great! I just want people to be healthier and feel their best…while taking ownership for their health. Unfortunately, many of these programs are short term fixes without modification of underlying unhealthy behaviors. As long as there is a need, these programs will continue to be available and more will continue to pop up. The important thing is that they are safe and cause no harm.

Trend #5: There will be continued dwindling of physician insurance reimbursement & higher premiums for patients

As with many specialties, physician reimbursement is on the decline within the bariatric field and some services are just not covered. A great influence is the Affordable Care Act and the federal government lowering Medicare reimbursement rates. When this happens, private insurance companies tend to follow suit. Not only are they lowering physician reimbursement rates, but the federal government is also moving towards a flat reimbursement rate regardless of the complexity of the patient's condition.[6] This ultimately affects payment for hospitals and physicians alike. It can also negatively affect patient care.

As you know (all too well) with this model, in order to remain solvent, the volume of visits/procedures needs to increase in the same amount of time. Thus, there is less time to spend with patients and potentially higher complications/readmission rates among other negative outcomes. As an end result, stress overtakes the enjoyment of caring for patients (which has already happened in many facets of healthcare) and contributes to physician burnout which negatively affects quality of care as well.

Trend #6: There will be an increase in concierge cash pay medically supervised weight loss programs (with the Proper Mindset & Marketing Plan)

There is more than one way to implement your medical weight loss program which we will explore shortly. In the meantime, one of the most popular is a concierge cash pay model. This model requires the proper mindset for sales and exceeding patient expectations. It also requires a great marketing plan because you need to effectively identify and attract those that are willing to pay for this individualized and specialized care.

Implementing a cash pay medical weight loss for your patients can be a very positive game changer for your business. There is a sub-population of patients seeking such services but they come with specific expectations (and often a bit more determination and motivation). Cash pay services in a variety of specialties is becoming much more common. These include plastic surgery/aesthetics, orthopedic services and, as you likely know, concierge family practice settings. If you already have one of these programs, you are poised perfectly to add cash pay medical weight loss to your practice.

Here are a few important cash pay insights that I have observed while managing a self-pay medical weight loss program:

Patient Benefits:

- Freedom of choice
- Viable option for those that don't have insurance coverage
- Higher motivation with some 'skin in the game'
- Individualized care
- Comprehensive services

Practice:

- Higher profit margin
- No time required for staff to obtain insurance authorizations
- No time required for staff to perform billing/collection activities
- Self-pay patients are often more motivated. This enhances enjoyment of patient care and improves patient outcomes

Patient Risks:

- Higher out of pocket expense

Practice Risks:

- Must be sure that self-pay services are in compliance with insurance guidelines or completely separated and offered through an entity that does not participate with insurance
- Requires effective management of patient expectations and true 'sales' for patient acquisition.

The benefits tend to outweigh the risks. Thus, having a self-pay option for your weight loss patients can be very helpful. However, depending upon your patient demographic, you need to know that it can be difficult to find patients interested in self-pay. The most successful practices are those that are able to focus on creating a program that includes what these patients desire most.

Experience shows this clientele completes very thorough research and desire the following:

- Experienced practitioners with a history of excellent outcomes and positive reviews
- Cost effective package price and/or cost effective 'pay as you go' option
- Personalized, professional and friendly service in a warm environment
- Concierge style care with seamless care delivery
- Clear communication
- Ongoing comprehensive support that is convenient and proven effective

Thus, when creating your self-pay program, addressing each of these elements is critical.

The next step is to utilize marketing strategies that engage patients. Often non-traditional marketing measures work best such as online efforts along with some traditional marketing to pique interest. You need to build a relationship with them so they choose to invest in themselves through you. This is conveyed online as well as from the first phone call or interaction with your office staff. It is absolutely critical that each step is addressed and monitored closely for process improvement opportunities.

Trend #7: Medical weight loss practices will have a need for additional practice revenue streams

It is no surprise that with dwindling government and private insurance payments, medical weight loss practices/programs need to diversify and create additional revenue streams that complement their services. This may feel adverse to some but such revenue streams actually complement all types of medical weight loss programs and have been shown to improve patient outcomes. The most effective and appropriate options for consideration at this time include:

1. Retail (Vitamins & Nutritional Supplements)
2. Medications
3. Fitness
4. Back on Track services for long term patients who may be struggling

If you haven't added any of these additional products/services to your program, you will find that patients not only desire such services but they are beginning to expect them. In addition, with proper guidance and planning, they are easier to add than you may think.

Trend #8: Patient expectations will continue to rise when paying for concierge medical weight loss

Concierge medicine is defined in Wikipedia as "a relationship between a patient and a primary care physician in which the patient pays an annual fee or retainer. This may or may not be in addition to other charges."[7] However, it is so much more than that! It is your relationship with your patient and your intent/desire to streamline their care so it is efficient, convenient and personalized. This doesn't mean let them run all over you and make unrealistic demands. In fact, that rarely happens as long as expectations are managed up front and communication is clear each step of the way.

These expectations are becoming more of the norm. When you think about it, isn't that what you would desire for your patient care experience? You may think such desires are more like unnecessary demands. However, when proper systems are put in place for customer service, phone etiquette, online presence, testimonial gathering, coordinated care pathways, patient communication and the like, it becomes easier to manage and more enjoyable for all.

Trend #9: There will be an increased focus on clean eating and environmental friendly options for patients

Did you know that Millennials are now the largest population group? They actually outnumber Baby Boomers.[3] Although more common among all ages nowadays, many Millennials tend to prefer clean eating in addition to convenience. Thus, having weight loss meal options that include whole foods as a part of your program is important. Having retail products conveniently available that are gluten free without artificial ingredients will be of interest as well.

2

RISKS/BENEFITS OF ADDING MEDICAL
WEIGHT LOSS TO YOUR PRACTICE

One thing you can always count on from me is honesty and transparency. I understand what it is like to start a new endeavor when others think you are crazy. I know what it is like to have abundance and really cool growth which is great! I also know what it is like to put your heart and soul into something and see it blossom...so...slowly. So slowly in fact, that you have to check your bank account each day before you pay your bills, reassure yourself every day you are doing the right thing, question yourself and pray you can take care of your employees who are like family to you...as well as your own family. You see, my husband is a visionary and I am the 'go to gal' that builds the team along with systems and makes it happen. We love, we trust, we care, we have faith and we persevere. However, we definitely know the ups and downs of being entrepreneurs and fortunately, there have been more ups than downs.

We love, we trust, we care,
we have faith and we persevere.

As I talk to physicians contemplating adding medical weight loss to their practice or starting an independent medical weight loss office, they tend to share some common fears which I will include as perceived risks in this section. Let's face it, what is perceived as real is real to the individual. I will explore these risks along with the benefits of adding medical weight loss to your practice below:

Potential/Perceived Risks:

1. Being viewed as another tycoon trying to make a buck with a weight loss program:

    > This may be a fear, but is actually YOUR issue unless that is really your intent and I suspect that is not the case.

2. Having to be a 'salesperson':

    > The beauty of medical weight loss is that the physician is not (nor should they be) the salesperson. You create raving fans that sell for you and send you more referrals. In the office, your trained staff should be doing the selling. Not you. If they believe in what you are doing and they see positive results, it doesn't feel like selling. They are helping others improve their health and that feels great!

3. Lack of need or desire within your community to participate in your weight loss program:

    > The need is real…just review the statistics shared earlier. If patients aren't purchasing from you, they are purchasing from someone else who is often less qualified.

4. Increased liability:

    The liability is there, just like any services offered by physicians. It is covered through your malpractice insurance just as other services you offer.

5. Too costly to implement:

    You can make adding medical weight loss services as expensive or inexpensive as you desire. In fact, there are some turn-key programs that can be implemented within a couple of weeks that create a return on investment and profit almost immediately.

6. Too much of a time commitment to implement:

    As with any new service offering, there is a time commitment for implementation. Delegation to staff helps and identifying a 'lead' person for the project helps to streamline things. Once systems are in place, this time commitment eases up and the focus can be moved to revenue generation and growth of the program.

7. Potential competition with colleagues in the field:

    With an abundance mindset, competition is viewed as a good thing. The reality is that there are plenty of overweight patients that desperately need what you are offering.

8. Non-reimbursable/Poor return on investment:

    You can choose to use insurance or build out a cash pay program. Either one, when set up properly will result in payment and profitability.

9. Lack of staff interest/buy-in:

    This can be a very real stumbling block. You will need to include them in setting up the program and set clear expectations. My experience is that they will rise to the occasion. Most staff is excited and you will likely find the health of your entire office improves.

10. Lack of experience:

    You can utilize turn-key programs that come with instruction and are proven effective. You can also obtain education through your national organization at a training course. You can gain experience quickly.

11. Failure:

    Like everything in life, failure is a possibility. However, follow your gut feelings, follow the processes outlined in this book and see the possibilities/realities unfold.

Potential Benefits:

1. More patients:

    With success comes more referrals.

2. More revenue:

    A new service brings more revenue and adding retail really boosts your bottom line!

3. Improved/resolved patient co-morbidities:

    Weight loss results in improvement and often resolution of co-morbidities.

4. Better patient health:

    Less co-morbidities and less weight improves patient health.

5. Happier patients:

    Successful patients make happy patients.

6. Happier staff:

    Seeing patients succeed makes everyone happy.

7. More referrals:

    Successful weight loss patients send their friends and family who want/need the same.

8. Improved quality of life:

    Better outcomes, increased revenue, improved quality of life for you and your patients.

9. Success:

    Is a huge potential benefit and something that IS attainable.

I know, I am often called an optimist. However, I am confident about the benefits of adding medical weight loss to your practice because I have seen the positive results firsthand. Although there are 11 risks and 9 benefits, I believe you can see that some of the risks are actually benefits in disguise.

If you have questions or want to toss around a few ideas, feel free to reach out to me at Karol@ WeightLossPracticeBuilder.com or schedule time to chat at www.smarturl.it/bookkarol.

3

YOUR BIG ADVANTAGE

Primary care physicians have a BIG advantage. In fact, any physician with an existing patient base is at an advantage. YOU have a built in clientele of patients who know, like and trust you. Of these, typically 2/3 of them need to lose weight. Who better to help them than YOU and your competent staff? This is one of those great business situations where proper marketing to your existing patients can result in a boost of medical weight loss patient's right from the start. You can also proactively partner with bariatric surgeons to assist them with the medical weight loss counseling often required for their patients pre-operatively in addition to provide support as necessary after weight loss surgery.

Bariatric surgeons have quite an advantage as well. You have patients call your office or visit your website every day that are not interested in weight loss surgery, are not candidates for weight loss surgery or do not have insurance coverage and cannot cover the self-pay cost for bariatric surgery. You have patients that could be entered into a medical weight loss program instead. Often surgeons ask me if these patients are likely to later convert to a weight loss surgery patient. The reality is that a few will. It is not really the percentage you may think. Most patients come through the door having done a great deal of research and want one or the other. They almost compartmentalize themselves into one category or the other. There will be a few that will gain trust and move to surgery but that is not the majority. By the same token, some will come in for their mandated medical weight loss program as a requirement for surgery and do so well, they continue on and decide not to have surgery. This is a fairly small percentage though (approximately 1%).

You simply have to decide if you are going to create your own program or implement/license use of a turn-key program that includes training. Usually marketing materials such as e-mail sequences, posters, media kits and letters to area physicians are also a part of the established program. You just make the decision and follow the established steps of implementation.

Or, if you prefer to create your own program right from the start, follow the steps outlined in this book and you will be on your way!

If you choose to add retail in your office as well (which has been shown to improve patient outcomes), your patients will notice and actually ask YOU for information about your weight loss program often before you have a chance to discuss it with them. In fact, we have turn-key retail programs as well or you can choose to research the various nutraceutical companies and do it on your own – your choice.

This is a win-win situation for you and your patients and pretty exciting!

4

STEP 1 – DO YOUR RESEARCH & CREATE YOUR VISION

Building something new (or renovating something older) is exciting. Sometimes we can get caught up with what we want and impatiently move forward prior to thinking it through. I agree that most successful people are decisive people. However, with a little preparation and guidance you can avoid much of the anxiety that comes with something new and move forward with greater confidence.

I believe that when someone says they are 'experienced' what they really mean is that they went through a lot of trial and error. They made mistakes which taught them lessons along the way. I know I have made my share of mistakes in order to become 'experienced' and I would like to help you avoid making some of the same ones.

Your first step is to do your research by asking yourself and your team a few questions:

1. What is your vision?
2. What services do you want to offer initially? What additional services do you want to offer over time?
3. Do you have established patients interested in what you want to offer?
4. Who is your primary competition for your new offering?
5. What resources do you have in your current office to provide such services?
6. What resources will you need?
7. Is there a medical weight loss program in existence you like and would a site visit be helpful?

These questions are pretty straight forward. As you go through this book, some of the answers will become clear and others will require a little bit of time and effort.

I am going to address vision because this sets the tone for what you create and is often under-estimated. It is the vision that everyone on your team needs to be able to understand so they know what they are working towards. This needs to come from the top down and preferably from the physician(s) if possible. They respect you and they want to do a good job. You make it easier for them to be creative and do their job well if they understand your vision.

I am not sure if you are a Stephen Covey fan or not but his advice applies extremely well to creating your weight loss program and life in general. Dr. Covey states that Begin with the End in Mind means to begin each day, task or project with a clear vision of your desired direction and destination and then continue by flexing your proactive muscles to make things happen.[8] This vision is what should drive your decisions and actions related to the design of your building/internal space, your furnishings, your décor, selection of your staff, patient population and services you offer to name a few. You may choose to visit other programs and see what they are doing but then it is important to make it your own vision with what you feel is the best of the best for you and those you serve.

Don't be afraid to use your imagination and think about how you can use the present to prepare for the future. Many thought we were crazy to put medical, surgical, fitness and retail weight loss services under one roof. Actually we started to doubt the idea (well I did, my husband never had that thought) and yet, our model has been duplicated in other cities and is now becoming the new standard.

> *Don't be afraid to use your imagination and think about how you can use the present to prepare for the future.*

Here is an example of what our vision entailed and what we shared with our team:

We will create a comprehensive, state of the art weight loss center that includes adequate space for education, events, counseling, fitness, retail, staff support, exam/treatment and storage. The design will be non-traditional with an open, warm, 'groovy', unique, clean and organized yet inviting feel that showcases patient success. Our staff will be friendly, efficient, self-directed, optimistic, creative, skilled, dedicated, loyal and sensitive to patient needs. Our office and staff will support healthy habits with adherence to the same types of foods we encourage our patient to eat (of course special occasions excluded!). The staff will be rewarded for their dedication and have full access to the services we offer our patients in addition to products in the nutritional store available at cost. Our logo and brand will exude positivity, hope, success and a strong relationship with our patients. Communication will be clear and services offered in a concierge style. Our patient education will be thorough and available onsite as well as fully available on mobile devices for patient convenience.

This vision drove our design decisions for an open style front desk, warm colors for décor, specific facility planning/design including some angled walls to enhance an open feel rather than a boxed look. There is soft lighting and sconces on the walls to create an elegant and yet comfortable feel. Chairs have no arms and match the décor along with classic/contemporary furniture in the waiting room/bathrooms and classroom. Patient success stories adorn all spaces. Bright customized posters with professional patient photos and their quotes are placed strategically throughout the office on the walls. The computers all have wireless keypads and desks have little clutter. The fitness center has a private training area, access 5am-10pm and equipment that can accommodate persons of any size. The equipment is also easy to use with clear explanation and a video from one of the trainers available for each circuit machine via a simple QR code. The floor is designed to absorb pressure and ease jarring of joints. On their own, the staff tends to have a protein shake for breakfast in the morning and follow primarily the same regimen as the patients. They are apt to share recipes they create and utilize the fitness center when they can.

Think about what you want for your center. You may not need any changes at all and that is ideal!! I do not recommend adding a lot of cost before the program even gets off the ground. In fact, the description above may sound overwhelming. Believe me, we have come a long way – we had a similar "feel" in our old building which was simply a renovated 7-11 building with terrible parking. Be creative with your space and program offerings. Make it something you are excited and proud to share with your patients.

If your plans involve new construction, select your builder carefully. Interview them and make sure if possible there is a foreman on site. This will help as you tour your new facility during construction and find things that require slight modifications or attention. Sometimes what is on the architectural plans looks a bit different once under construction. If you can avoid expensive renovations or new construction, I highly recommend that. Wait until you have things flowing smoothly and then make such changes with money saved from profits without adding a great amount of debt. Personally, I love facility planning. If you desire an honest opinion, feel free to reach out to me at Karol@WeightLossPracticeBuilder.com.

5

STEP 2 – DETERMINE YOUR BUSINESS MODEL & KEY PROGRAM COMPONENTS

As you determine your business model, your primary decision will be whether you are going to bill insurance for services rendered or establish a cash pay/fee for service model. This is a business and personal decision.

Understand that as you consider your decision, there is a dichotomy at play. Most patients would like to use their insurance and most physicians prefer self-pay since it is cash up front and no added expense to file with insurance and follow up on billing/collections. For patients, using insurance is considered advantageous, especially for those with Medicare and Affordable Care Act policies which have no co-pay. Patients with commercial insurances that have higher co-pays may prefer cash pay because in some instances, the amount paid per visit will be lower than their co-pay, especially if bundled into a package price.

Business Models:

1. Cash Pay/Fee for Service:

   This is the simplest model to implement because you are paid as services are provided or paid in advance for packaged services. The obstacle for many is the ability to sell such services to those that feel as if they should be able to use their insurance for such care. This is simplified with sales training, scripts and bundling highly valued services and products into your offer. The more your staff believes in your products and services, the easier it will be for them to sell with enthusiasm and confidence to prospective patients.

   I am not a healthcare attorney or insurance specialist so I strongly suggest you do your own research and discuss with your counsel the requirements and recommendations for your corporation and tax ID when it comes to interpretation of your insurance agreements.

   If you are starting a new medical weight loss clinic and choose to follow the cash pay model, it is easiest to obtain a new tax ID number, not accept insurance for this entity from the very beginning and never bill any insurance company for services rendered. Your patient documentation for financial agreements and consent to care needs to reflect this as well. Again, obtain counsel from your professional team for specific requirements.

   Setting up your fee structure can be overwhelming and confusing. You want to be paid for your expertise and concierge services, yet you don't want to outprice your marketplace. However, I *do not* recommend you be the cheapest game in town. People are willing to pay for results, expertise, exclusivity and customized services. In addition, they tend to do better if they have some 'skin in the game'. Remember, you need to be able to not only cover your costs, but operate with a positive bottom line in order to grow your practice and make a living.

You will likely modify your fee structure somewhat over time. You will get a feel for what people are willing to pay and as you begin your sales process, you will also tweak your sales pitch and offers.

You know patients need counseling/accountability and you know they need education. However, patients just want results. Many are wary of paying for 'education' and 'counseling'. However, it is amazing how willing they are to spend money on something they can touch and feel like great tasting nutritional products, vitamins, medications, injections, personal training, cups, gadgets and the like. Even 'coaching' instead of 'counseling' tends to be easier to sell because it feels more concrete.

As you create your pricing structure, you will want to consider the components you want to include in your medical weight loss program (also discussed in this chapter). At the end of this chapter is a sample of a cash pay program option along with pricing that has been proven to sell at our office. I have also helped implement variations at other offices as well depending upon their clientele and needs. One thing I have found to be true is that the simpler your options are the better. If you give people too many choices, they are often unable to make a choice. They will get confused and leave your office without ever making a decision.

It is critical to remain true to your core values, beliefs and training. You will be approached by many sales representatives to offer the next best thing available for weight loss and patients will want to see you just for appetite suppressants without any other services. It can be easy to go down this 'revenue hole' but in the end, do what feels right to you. For example, our phone rings every day with someone asking if they can just get an appetite suppressant. Our physician will not prescribe an appetite suppressant (Schedule III or IV medications nonetheless) without them being in one of our programs and having ongoing counseling. They also have to have a normal EKG on file and have attempted our diet plan first. If they still feel as if their appetite is not under control (with proper low carb/adequate protein diets, appetite tends to be naturally suppressed) then he will evaluate them for an appetite suppressant. Yes, we lose potential patients but this is what we feel is best for the patient.

2. Insurance

The primary belief I hear from many healthcare providers is that you cannot get paid for weight loss services through insurance. This is true in cases such as when you have someone provide the services that are not an approved provider with the insurance company (i.e. personal trainer or nutritionist). This is also true if you bill for such services through a non-eligible specialty or non-eligible place of service (POS). Other obstacles to payment include improper coding, diagnosis, incomplete documentation or lack of coverage for obesity services as determined through insurance verification for benefits and eligibility.

At the time of this publication, Medicare guidelines identify the following as eligible specialties for billing weight loss services[9]:

- 01 – General Practice
- 08 – Family Practice
- 11 – Internal Medicine
- 16 – Obstetrics/Gynecology
- 37 – Pediatric Medicine
- 38 – Geriatric Medicine
- 50 – Nurse Practitioner
- 89 – Certified Clinical Nurse Specialist
- 97 – Physician Assistant

At the time of this publication, it is noted that for obesity counseling claims containing codes for obesity behavioral counseling services (HCPCS G0447/G0473), Medicare will only pay when such services are provided in one of the following Place of Service (POS) codes[9]:

- 11 – Physician's Office
- 22 – Outpatient Hospital
- 49 – Independent Clinic
- 71 – State or Local Public Health Clinic

If you are billing for weight loss services/ counseling or group counseling, I recommend you take one of the Obesity Coding courses offered through the Obesity Medicine Association (www. ObesityMedicine.org) and always check your payors' policies and guidelines as well as the AMA's CPT coding guidelines. The courses offered through the Obesity Medicine Association are inexpensive, thorough and will give you the latest accurate guidelines and tips for obtaining reimbursement.

Typically, the coding for obesity screening, treatment and counseling can include the following codes. In addition, obesity screening and counseling are time-based codes, (when counseling constitutes >50% of the face-to-face encounter). Thus, documentation of these services must include the amount of time spent with the patient:

- 99201-99205 – New Patient Evaluation and Management
- 99211-99215 – Established Patient Evaluation and Management
- 99381-99387 – Preventive Medicine – New Patient
- 99391-99397 – Preventive Medicine – Established Patient
- 99401-99405 – Preventive Medicine – Counseling Risk Factor Reduction
- 99406-99409 – Preventive Medicine – Behavior Change Intervention New or Established
- HCPCS Codes – G0447/G0473

There are many other requirements which can change frequently and of course, if medications are prescribed, this will increase the level of the E/M code.

If you are a primary care physician who currently accepts insurance and decide to add medical weight loss, you can always use E/M codes based upon the length of your visit along with appropriate documentation and supporting ICD-10 codes.

As an additional tip, if you are using HCPCS codes G0474 or G0473 for obesity screening and behavioral counseling, Medicare requires only the ICD-10, Z codes for BMI measurement. Without this code, the claim will typically be denied. For commercial payors, they require the primary obesity ICD-10, Z codes for BMI >30 and then you can use secondary obesity diagnosis codes such as E66.01, E66.09, E66.8 and E66.9.

You can experience success with either model. It is your choice. In my experience, the cash pay model is simpler to implement though and tends to be more profitable and satisfying in the long run – especially when offered with a retail store.

Program Components:

There is a fine balance between keeping your program offerings simple, yet enticing and saleable. I know from 'experience' (aka much trial and error), that the more complex your offers, the harder they will be to sell.

> *There is a fine balance between keeping
> your program offerings simple, yet enticing
> and saleable.*

Our team has worked hard to create compelling educational programs, effective coaching/accountability, ancillary services and retail products that truly help people lose weight, keep them coming back regularly and inspired to refer their friends/family. Our options range from 2 week programs to 6 month programs as well as 12 month programs for those undergoing bariatric surgery. Your goal is to help your patients experience immediate results for motivation and then keep them engaged and accountable so their success continues.

Key Components of a Successful Medical Weight Loss Program:

In my experience and those I work with, that the most important components to include in your medical weight loss program for optimal patient outcomes includes:

Education:

Initially, education can be provided with simple handouts utilized at coaching sessions. If this continues to work well for you, then you can continue with this method.

We found that over time, we wanted to formalize much of the educational materials we had created. We ended up putting it into a curriculum called Weight Management University™. This program is now accessible online through a private membership site and includes video, audio and written chapters complete with assignments and specific instructions that is reinforced through coaching sessions. Each module is available as soon as someone signs up for the program and is also 'dripped' to them through their e-mail over a 6 month period as a reminder (and reinforced during one on one coaching visits). In addition to quite a bit of bonus material such as fitness videos, recipes, journals and the like, the following educational modules are included for the participating patient (below are direct patient descriptions of each module):

1. **Getting Started & Goal Setting:** Motivation happens with quick results. This module shows you how to maximize your investment with quick implementation and weight loss to keep you going. Learn what you can begin today and the top thing you need to focus on – no need to feel overwhelmed.

2. **Accountability:** Setting up an accountability plan keeps you on track now and over time is critical to your success. This module shows you how without overwhelming you.

3. **The Basics—How to Get Results:** Dr. Clark's chapter on 'The Basics' teaches you what really counts when it comes to what you are eating. You will receive your personalized nutrition plan during your Metabolic/Diet evaluation with Dr. Clark. You will also learn the difference between "eating healthy" and "eating healthy to lose weight". Weight loss doesn't have to be complicated. Eating healthy made easy for you!

4. **Macronutrients:** This module teaches you what really counts when it comes to what you are eating. You will learn what you need to count for optimal success without overwhelming you with unnecessary

tracking you don't need to worry about. Includes your 1, 2, 3 plan that simplifies not only what you need to eat but how to stay satisfied.

5. **Supplements:** No need for confusion when it comes to the many vitamins and supplements available. This module clarifies what you need for optimal results. You will look and feel your best!

6. **Cardio Exercise/ NEAT:** Fitness that begins at your level. This module teaches you what you may not know about exercise and how to make it an enjoyable part of your routine.

7. **Eating In/Eating Out**: This module makes eating in and eating out a breeze. You will learn how to make your healthy choices with ease – no need to stress here!

8. **Carbohydrates:** The good, the bad and the ugly is simplified for you when it comes to eating carbohydrates. This module includes the information you must know for best results.

9. **Stress...less:** Stress – we all have it. You will learn how stress affects your body and your ability to lose weight. It also shows you the best ways to conquer your stress!

10. **Protein:** Protein is a misunderstood macronutrient. This module gives you the skinny on protein, staying satisfied and building the metabolism you desire.

11. **Resistance Training:** You will finally learn the fitness side of building your ideal metabolism – for weight loss and long term weight management. Don't miss this one!

12. **What about Fat?:** Fat is another very misunderstood macronutrient. You don't have to live in fear – learn what you do and don't want to eat when it comes to fat choices. Fat isn't necessarily making you fat!

13. **Micronutrients:** Vitamins are part of a healthy diet. Knowing what to look for in a quality supplement is important.

14. **Where do I go from here?:** You have lost weight, your blood sugar is under control, your activity has improved (and you actually look forward to it), your lean body mass is higher – don't lose your momentum – this module continues your plan for long-term success. No more yo-yo dieting for you!

As coaching sessions take place, each educational module is briefly reviewed along with patient food journals and a set assessment pattern that is customized to the needs of the patient. The counseling focus is behavior modification. Patients also have access to the physician each week during a live webinar as well as support through phone calls, e-mail and a private Facebook group. We get to know them very well.

Patients often don't think they need education but when delivered this way in addition to individualized coaching and the other components of the program, we are in contact with them frequently and they do not feel alone.

Creating interactive, engaging content (written, audio and video) to educate and support your patients has never been easier. You may already have some of these assets created. If not, don't worry, audio and video can easily be done yourself without a lot of 'tech'. Your smartphone and an app or software like Camtasia®, iMovie or Final Cut Pro for video does the trick and then within these programs you can separate the audio. Presto – you have audio for podcasts or for people to listen to on the go and video for those who learn visually in addition to any written materials.

> *Creating interactive, engaging content*
> *(written, audio and video) to education and*
> *support your patients has never been easier.*

Patients prefer that you be yourself so you don't have to stress that you need to be perfect. Bottom line, taking your educational program and packaging it online and/ or as written material with video and audio available for the mobile society will set you apart from your competition and can be the basis for your educational program. This engaging, ongoing education exemplifies your dedication to their long term success and makes you unique.

Accountability:

According to the Merriam-Webster dictionary, accountability is "an obligation or willingness to accept responsibility or to account for one's actions".[10] Yet, it seems as if we try to keep others accountable for their actions. The reality is that we coach, we counsel, we guide, we care and we hope those we serve will take our assistance to heart and become accountable. We actually cannot control their actions but we try so hard to show the benefits of a healthier life. Yet, it the end, it is up to them.

We have programs that are entirely online. Patients that are motivated, self-directed and accountable do very well. Those that are not flounder and tend to throw in the towel often saying that it is 'one more program that failed me' or 'just another program that didn't work'.

I am an optimist at heart but a few things I have learned over the years is that people need to take responsibility for their health, be accountable and be willing to do the work for ultimate success. Easier said than done, I know. Also, anything FREE isn't valued and is rarely followed through on. As a nurse, I always want to help and practically give everything away for free. I have learned that doesn't usually work well. I will not give up though. As you likely know, having that one person who comes out of their shell, gives you a HUGE smile or cries as they are able to finally lose weight and do every day activities that they haven't been able to do for years makes it all worth it.

Meal Plans:

Especially at the beginning, most patients just want you to tell them what to do. They want it simple and well outlined. If you prepare specific meal plans for your patients, they will usually be more compliant. As soon as something is confusing, it becomes hard and that becomes a potential barrier to continue with the program. An easy to follow meal plan that outlines what to eat and what not to eat will help aid in your patients' success.

A shopping list will help as well as weekly or monthly newsletters with easy to use recipes and meal plan variations. Your patients will be very appreciative if you include this as a part of your program.

Retail Products Onsite:

Chapter 9 outlines specifically how you can integrate retail products into your program. You have a number of choices. You can go with one vendor and whatever program they promote. This is simple.

However, as I will review in Chapter 9, in my opinion, very few vendors have cornered the market on taste or price for the various high quality vitamin and nutraceutical products patients want and need. We have found that it may take a little bit more time to set up, but patients are happier having a choice of quality products and your potential for revenue growth is much higher when you are not committed to just one vendor.

Recipes:

This is a great time to involve your dietician, nutritionist and/or staff. You will be amazed at what they come up with in addition to current recipes easily available to you online. You want to make sure recipes are in concert with your nutritional recommendations and include calories, protein and carbohydrate amounts. For us (and many medical weight loss programs), intake of carbohydrate is most important, then protein and total calories is a distant third.

Interestingly, we post recipes regularly on Pinterest and over time, it has been shown to be a great lead generation tool. People find our recipes and then want to know more about us and many eventually become patients.

Ongoing Support and Outcome Tracking:

Numbers matter. You just spent time creating a new program for your patients so you will want to track your numbers. You will want to compare patient outcomes at set times throughout your program and provide ongoing feedback to any other specialists involved in your patients care. You can also easily track patient feedback and satisfaction onsite at visits and through simple online questionnaires.

Tracking numbers is the easiest part. It is the engagement and ongoing effective support that poses the greatest challenge. Let's face it, people are busy and weight loss is a struggle for most. Or, your patients may be doing so well, they don't think they really need you or your awesome comprehensive program (even if they paid for it already).

Engagement comes from knowing what interests your patients and delivering that (while sneaking in exactly what they need). Some engagement strategies that we have found to be very helpful include:

- Scales that communicate to you your patients weight
- Regular e-mails with educational videos, recipes and the like
- Educational social media posts particularly on Facebook and Pinterest
- Dynamic membership site that tracks progress through educational materials
- MP3 files for patients to listen to in the car

- Weekly podcasts that patients can listen to while walking/working out
- Engaging fitness videos with the surgeon, staff and/ or personal trainers
- Unique fitness classes such as TRX, Strength Yoga, Barre and whatever is 'all the rage' at that particular moment in time along with certified instructors available to teach
- Office events in the store as well as support groups and cooking classes

When done well, patients become raving fans and readily refer others to you. From a marketing perspective, that's when strategies such as patient testimonials and a patient referral program will be helpful to implement.

Engagement comes from knowing what interests your patients and delivering that (while sneaking in exactly what they need).

Optional Medical Weight Loss Program Components Include:

Some other optional components that creat additional desirable/supportive services for your patients as well as additional revenue streams for you include:

Medications:

According to the Obesity Action Coalition, there are several medications that are approved by the FDA for weight-loss.[11] These approved medications are outlined with information directly from the Obesity Action Coalition[11] in the table below:

Drug	How Does It Work?	Weight Loss	Concerns
Phentermine (Adipex-P®, Lomaira®)	Phentermine is a medication available by prescription that works on chemicals in the brain to decrease your appetite. It also has a mild stimulant component that adds extra energy. Phentermine is a pill that is taken once a day in the morning time. Tolerance to this medication can develop, so it is often used for only several months at a time. Common side effects are dry mouth and sleeplessness.	The average weight-loss is 4-5 percent of your weight after one-year. In a 200 pound person, this means about 10 pounds of weight-loss.	Due to its stimulant effect, a person's blood pressure and heart rate may increase when on this medication; therefore, you must be monitored closely by a physician who is experienced in prescribing this medication. It cannot be used in patients with some heart conditions (such as poorly controlled blood pressure), glaucoma (increased pressure in your eye), stroke or overactive thyroid. There is some concern for abuse, but this is minimal if the medication is appropriately used as directed by a healthcare professional.

Drug	How Does It Work?	Weight Loss	Concerns
Orlistat (Xenical® or alli®)	The medication alli® is a lower potency of the prescription drug Xenical® (orlistat). It is the only FDA-approved weight-loss medication that is available over-the-counter and available at a higher dose with a prescription. It is a capsule that is usually taken three times per day before a meal that contains dietary fat. It works by decreasing the amount of fat your body absorbs. This means that only 2/3 of the calories that you take in from fat will be absorbed. The other 1/3 of the calories gets carried away in the digestion tract as stool. The company that makes this drug (GlaxoSmithKline Consumer Healthcare) also offers a Web site with education and support tools for users at www.myalli.com.	The average weight-loss is about 5 percent of your weight after one year. In a person who weighs 200 pounds, this would mean 10 pounds of weight-loss.	It does not work well for people who are already on a low-fat diet since their calories from fat are already low. Individuals using alli® on a regular basis should take a daily multivitamin as there is potential for deficiency in some vitamins. One of the advantages of alli® is that its side effects are limited to the gastrointestinal system. Common side effects are cramps, gas, stool leakage, oily spotting and gas with discharge that improve with a lower fat diet.

Drug	How Does It Work?	Weight Loss	Concerns
Lorcaserin HCI (Belviq®)	Lorcaserin HCl was approved in June 2012 by the FDA and became commercially available in June 2013. It works by helping you feel full while eating less, and it works on the chemicals in your brain to help decrease your appetite.	In individuals who took the medication for one-year, it has been shown to have an average of 7 percent weight-loss. In a 200 pound person, this would mean a 14 pound weight-loss. Blood sugar, cholesterol and blood pressure levels have also been shown to improve.	The most common side effects are headache, dizziness, fatigue, dry mouth, upper respiratory tract infection and nausea.
Naltrexone HCI AND Bupropion HCI (CONTRAVE®)	CONTRAVE®, approved in 2014 by the FDA, is a combination of two medications that have been approved for other medical problems. Naltrexone is a medication used for the treatment of narcotic and alcohol dependency. Bupropion is used as an antidepressant and for helping people stop smoking. When used in combination, these two medications work together in the brain to decrease appetite and control eating.	Among individuals who took the medication for one year, 65 percent of the study subjects lost at least 5 percent of their body weight. In a 200 pound person, this would mean a 10 pound weight-loss. Also, 39 percent lost at least 10 percent of their body weight. In a 200 pound person, this would mean a 20 pound weight-loss. Improvements in bad cholesterol, triglycerides and good cholesterol were also seen.	The common side effects are nausea, constipation, headache, dry mouth, vomiting and dizziness.

Drug	How Does It Work?	Weight Loss	Concerns
Phentermine-Topiramate ER (Qsymia®)	This combination medication was approved by the FDA in July 2012. Topiramate is a medication used in migraine prevention as well as seizure prophylaxis. It was found that a common side effect of this medication was weight-loss. Phentermine, as described in this brochure, helps to increase your energy and decrease your appetite.	Among individuals who took the highest does of Qsymia® (15 mg phentermine and 92 mg of topiramate ER) for one-year, they achieved an average of 14.4 percent weight-loss. In a 200 pound person, a 14.4 percent weight-loss would mean a loss of 29 pounds. Cholesterol levels have also been shown to improve.	The most common side effects were dry mouth, constipation and pins-and-needle feeling in extremities. Qsymia® should NOT be used in women of childbearing age who are not using at least one reliable form of contraception. Topiramate ER, a component of Qsymia®, has been known to cause birth defects.
Liraglutide injection (Saxenda®)	Liraglutide, approved in 2014 by the FDA, is an injectable medication that increases our natural production of insulin, which is needed to regulate the levels of sugar in the blood. It decreases the production of a hormone that opposes insulin called glucagon.	In four trials consisting of more than 5,000 individuals, participants received 3mg of liraglutide daily. The outcomes showed that among individuals who took the medication for one year, 73 percent of the study subjects lost at least 5 percent of their body weight.	The most common side effects are nausea, vomiting, diarrhea and constipation.

Drug	How Does It Work?	Weight Loss	Concerns
Liraglutide injection (Saxenda®)	It also slows down the emptying of the stomach. Lastly, it works in the brain to reduce the amount of food consumed. As such, it has been used for the management of diabetes for the last few years.	In a 200 pound person, this would mean a 10 pound weight-loss. Also, 41 percent lost at least 10 percent of their body weight. In a 200 pound person, this would mean a 20 pound weight-loss.	

If you choose to dispense medications through your office, there are very strict state guidelines. Be sure to follow those guidelines along with any required site visits and added licensure prior to ordering or dispensing any medications.

B-12 Injections:

B vitamins have been shown to potentially increase energy levels. In addition, Lipo-B-12 is a compounded intramuscular injectable that can also aid with mobilization of adipose fat. These injections have been around for quite some time and are believed to be very safe.

Patients seek such injections and tout their benefits. Adding this to your service offerings can prove to increase patient satisfaction and generate additional revenue for your practice.

Retail Products Online:

In addition to on-site retail sales, it can be fairly easy to set up an online e-store and even complete your own fulfillment/distribution. This is not necessary right away or at all, but can be of benefit as a way to capture additional retail sales, especially for patients that may have moved from your area. In fact, as you have promotional sales, many systems allow for online sales with an option to pick up at the office. This is very satisfying for the customer because it streamlines their buying experience since their products are paid for and ready to go when they stop by.

We also have a patient rewards program whereby patients earn money each time they make a purchase. Patients love this feature as well as our monthly nutrition store parties and specials.

Fitness Classes/Personal Training:

Fitness can be provided as group exercise with someone on your staff or an experienced contracted group exercise instructor. Patients tend to enjoy coming to your office so offering such classes can be very beneficial and keep them connected to you and your offerings. It is not necessary but a nice addition to your program.

You can also contract with a personal trainer and have them meet with your patients at least once during their program. This is an added benefit that may set you apart from your competition. You can roll the cost into your program price.

Complementary Medical Weight Loss Program Components:

Some physicians consider these services potentially on the 'fringe' of their comfort zone. However, they have been integrated quite effectively into many medical weight loss programs. I wouldn't start with these but as your practice continues to grow with a larger number of raving fans, they often desire even more services from you. These should only be considered if it fits into your personal level of comfort, if adequate training/certifications are obtained and if they fit into your business plan. The last thing you want to do is have a successful business and then introduce a service that ends up draining your profits because it is not set up properly, promoted properly or well received by staff and patients alike.

Aesthetic Services:

This may be a little out on the fringe for many physicians but has been shown to be successful in some medical weight loss practices. Such services can be as simple as massage or some physicians add an aesthetician or other related services/retail.

Bio-Identical Hormone Replacement Therapy:

This may be an odd service to suggest but we have found it to be a very complimentary service that our patients actually requested. Contact me if you are interested in learning more at Karol@WeightLossPracticeBuilder.com.

As promised, below is a sample cash-pay medical weight loss program (front and back side of flier). This is just one example used at our center for our Weight Management University™ program. In fact, you can access this document online at http://cdn.cfwls.com/content/uploads/2018/03/ WMU-6-month-2018.pdf. There are other examples outlined in Chapter 11.

WEIGHTLOSS SUCCESS

Your Weight Management University™ curriculum takes you step-by-step through the process of losing weight, and more importantly, how to keep it off for life! Combine this with your personalized diet plan, individual counseling, lifestyle classes and fitness program and you have everything you need to make your goals a reality of weight loss success!

In addition to the modules below and the many bonuses already included, your Members Only portal is filled with fitness tips/videos, tasty recipes and inspiration to keep you motivated.

Core Modules	Includes 14 Chapters & Corresponding Videos
1. Getting Started & Goal Setting	Motivation happens with quick results. This module shows you how to maximize your investment with quick implementation and weight loss to keep you going. Learn what you can begin today and the top thing you need to focus on – no need to feel overwhelmed!
2. Accountability	Setting up an accountability plan keeps you on track now and over time is critical to your success. This module shows you how without overwhelming you.
3. The Basics—How to Get Results	Dr. Clark's chapter on "The Basics" teaches you what really counts when it comes to what you are eating. You will receive your personalized nutrition plan during your Metabolic/Diet evaluation with Dr. Clark. You will also learn the difference between "eating healthy" and "eating healthy for your weight". Weight loss doesn't have to be complicated. Eating healthy made easy for you!
4. Macronutrients	This module teaches you what really counts when it comes to what you are eating. You will learn what you need to count for optimal success without overwhelming you with unnecessary tracking you don't need to worry about. Includes your 1, 2, 3 plan that simplifies not only what you need to eat but how to stay satisfied.
5. Supplements	No need for confusion when it comes to the many vitamins and supplements available. This module clarifies what you need for optimal results. You will look and feel your best!
6. Cardio Exercise/ NEAT	Fitness that begins at your level. This module teaches you what you may not know about exercise and how to make it an enjoyable part of your routine.
7. Eating In/Eating Out	This module makes eating in and eating out a breeze. You will learn how to make your healthy choices with ease – no need to stress here!
8. Carbohydrates	The good, the bad and the ugly is simplified for you when it comes to eating carbohydrates. This module includes the information you must know for best results.
9. Stress...less	Stress – we all have it. You will learn how stress affects your body and your ability to lose weight. It also shows you the best ways to conquer your stress!
10. Protein	Protein is a misunderstood macronutrient. This module gives you the skinny on protein, staying satisfied and building the metabolism you desire.
11. Resistance Training	You will finally learn the fitness side of building your ideal metabolism – for weight loss and long term weight management. Don't miss this one!
12. What about Fat?	Fat is another very misunderstood macronutrient. You don't have to live in fear – learn what you do and don't want to eat when it comes to fat choices. Fat isn't necessarily making you fat!
13. Micronutrients	Vitamins are part of a healthy diet. Knowing what to look for in a quality supplement is important.
14. Where do I go from here?	You have lost weight, your blood sugar is under control, your activity has improved (and you actually look forward to it), your lean body mass is higher – don't lose your momentum – this module continues your plan for long-term success. No more yo-yo dieting for you!

6

STEP 3 – IDENTIFY YOUR RESOURCES/
JOIN OBESITY MEDICINE ASSOCIATION

When a new service is offered at a practice, I often find physicians and administrators wanting to add many new resources to ensure success and avoid stressing existing staff/systems. I fully understand this train of thought and how tempting it is. However, as someone who is dedicated to outstanding patient care and a positive bottom line, I find this is often not necessary. Some considerations for keeping your start-up costs low include:

- Take a look at your current team. See if you can identify someone who is interested in leading implementation of your medical weight loss endeavor. This is ideally someone with a clinical background who can work with your office manager/ administrator and you to make sure all bases are covered. It is amazing how, when presented with a new project, team members will rise to the occasion and take great pride in helping you build a new program. This is especially true with medical weight loss because it is something that will help improve the health of your staff as well as your patients. In addition, utilizing existing staff that your patients know, like and trust often helps with introduction of the new service to them.

• Make the most of resources available to you for best implementation practices. Use this book as a guide and consider utilization of turn-key programs for quicker and easier implementation/promotion as described in Chapter 11.

• Join the Obesity Medicine Association (www. obesitymedicine.org). Take one of their online courses or attend one of their conferences. Network and get involved.

• Consider board certication through American Board of Obesity Medicine.

• If you find you do need additional professional staff, consider contracting their services initially or bringing them on part-time until your new service is up and busy enough to warrant additional staff hours.

In the next chapter, I will cover some team building insights related to hiring, firing, benefits and team skill development. In the end, you want the right number of people on your team, the right team personality/skillset and a team that is dedicated to patient and business success. Perhaps you already have your dream team. If not, this information will help you build such a team. Once in place, you want to minimize turnover, maximize loyalty and reward them for a job well done.

7

STEP 4 – SURROUND YOURSELF WITH GREAT PEOPLE, TRAIN THEM AND TREAT THEM WELL

As you build your business, you will drive yourself crazy (and limit your success) if you try to do everything yourself. You must surround yourself with a competent, loyal, self-directed and motivated team. This includes your key employees along with your advisory team (corporate attorney, accountant, investment advisor, marketing specialist and coach/mentor). You may have a desire to cut corners here to save money. However, in the long run, you will actually spend more money due to staff turnover and potentially costly mistakes or "spinning your wheels" while getting nowhere fast.

I am one of those people who like to figure everything out and do it myself because then I know it is done right (or so I thought). I used to micro-manage our team (which drove everyone crazy) and then I started to delegate…with trepidation. Something I should have done a lot sooner. You see, I found that by micro-managing, I was limiting the creativity of our team, discouraging them from problem solving, limiting their ability to grow and preventing myself from becoming a true leader. To make matters worse, I was spending little quality time at home with my husband and 4 children because I was so "busy". While the business was still doing quite well, another outcome was stagnation of business growth and less joy. I micro-managed because of my perfectionist personality and also because of fear...fear of losing control and discovering that someone else might do it better – crazy I know!

Once I trusted the wonderful team we had built and challenged them with desired outcomes instead of tasks, they rose to the occasion...and are much happier. They work hard and we reward them accordingly. This has afforded me the opportunity to build my consulting business along with 2 additional businesses. I can actually relax knowing that processes and people are in place to keep the center moving in the right direction with a focus on stability and growth along with above average patient outcomes and satisfaction.

> *Once I trusted the wonderful team we had built and challenged them with desired outcomes instead of tasks, they rose to the occasion...and are much happier.*

So how do you build your dream team? This comes from your hiring process and your commitment to the fact that "everyone is replaceable". I am not cold hearted and actually we have a negligible turnover rate. If a position opens up it is usually for one of three reasons: someone is moving, someone has been nurtured through the practice to move beyond their role and has advanced to a new job (more on this later) or they aren't a good fit (which is preferably discovered during their orientation phase). Of course we follow employment rules and regulations, but we aren't afraid to document and discipline up to and including discharge if necessary. Fortunately, these instances are few and far between.

If you are in a large healthcare system and do not have a choice in your employee selection, I would challenge the precedent. Your staff is that important! As you know, they are your representative and your ambassadors. They are your first impression on most occasions. They are the ones who can prevent or instigate an unhappy patient. They are critical to an office that is enjoyable and an office that is productive (or not).

Where you find great employees varies. In my experience, I have found my best employees via word of mouth. On occasion I have found a great employee through an online advertisement but never through a temp agency. However, your experience may be different. Fortunately, I have a number of employees who have been with us since we moved to the area 23 years ago. They are that loyal, reliable and awesome.

Other important aspects to building a great team include:

- Take the time to meet with your staff and find out what their long term goals are. If possible, you should help them grow and support their further education. If you are a new manager to a practice, this is a great way to get to know your staff better and let them know you are interested and care.

- Match your team interests and skills to the needs of your business. If you have someone who has a great eye for design and is creative, you may want to give them additional training for graphic design, video editing and social media management. This way, you save cost for outside professionals and can have ready-made marketing materials, fliers and online posts ready to go much quicker than waiting for someone to get around to your project. It has NEVER been easier than now to create great looking graphics, edit video and launch online membership sites. This trend will likely continue. It is something my team and I love to do and makes it easier to catch testimonials 'live' and share new offerings in an instant to our patients and members of our community.

- Make sure you complete employee performance appraisals. This is a great time for you to share what is going well and what may need improvement along with determining goals for the next year. I will have staff fill out a questionnaire before we meet so I can see where they feel their strengths lie, what their areas for improvement are and what goals they have for themselves personally or professionally. Often you will find they are ready to take on additional responsibilities and this is a great way to help them grow and perhaps take a burden off of yourself or assist with a new project you have been thinking about.

- Always be fair. Playing favorites will get you into trouble and undermine staff respect for you.

- Follow through on what you say you will do. People need to know they can trust you.

- Find ways to recognize and reward your staff. A thank you verbally or with a personal note means more than you know. Remembering birthdays is also a nice touch as well as staff employment anniversaries.

- Team build in creative ways whether it is a quick game at work, "Spooking" them with candy at Halloween, a Christmas celebration or running a 5K together. These activities go a long way. It is fun to also create photos you can post on Facebook. This actually increases engagement with patients.

- We actually create job contracts for each position that the employee needs to sign. It is a job description that is written as a contract and requires a signature. It mandates a review of responsibilities and reinforces the importance of following through on each and every one.

As you know by now, your team is critical. They can make the difference between great days at work and days you got nothing done because you felt like you were babysitting teens or toddlers. Your example goes a long way. Be kind, be consistent, be firm when necessary and don't forget to say thank you.

8

STEP 5 – CREATE YOUR BUSINESS PLAN AND BUDGET

Writing a thorough business plan is essential if you are seeking financing. It may also surprise your banker since I have been told that many businesses don't take the time to create a well written document that 'sells' your project. I can say that every bank we approached was willing to lend and it was primarily based upon our comprehensive business plan.

Key components of your business plan includes an executive summary, biography/curriculum vitae for the borrower(s), personal financial statement if you are the personal guarantor, personal tax documents and/or business tax documents for the previous 3 years, revenue history for the previous 3 years if available, projected start-up costs and projected profitability schedule for the next 3 years.

Even if you are not seeking financing, having an active business plan will help guide your decisions and goals. At the very minimum, you need to create a budget for any construction/start-up costs and a budget for your first year in business. Your budget needs to include at least your projected revenue (including major sources from various cost centers), minus your cost of goods sold (COGS) for net revenue. Then identify your direct and indirect expenses and subtract from your net revenue for your final projected profit/loss.

Even if you are not seeking financing, having an active business plan will help guide your decisions and goals.

Sharing your financial goals with your staff is your decision. At the very least, your team needs to have volume goals and understand that they play a key role in the success of the business. This increases their buy in and commitment to meet or exceed the goals. Each and every employee is a critical cog in the wheel that determines if you travel smoothly or if your wheel breaks down and eventually crashes the car (your business).

My philosophy is that more information is better. I involve my management team in the initial annual/ quarterly planning of volume and revenue goals. Then I fine tune these goals and they are shared with the staff. There have been times that we have used a profit share model but at the moment, they are rewarded with a bonus when the business meets/exceeds financial goals.

For the retail store, your staff needs to know exact revenue goals. You will find that they have a tendency to become obsessed with meeting or exceeding them. This is awesome! As a result, they may throw in a surprise special in order to drive sales. I used to direct all promotions and sales but soon found out that it is better to let them create the promotion and I just provide helpful brainstorming and approval. We have been doing this for a long time. Over the years, I have discovered that they tend do better when you get out of the way!

9

STEP 6 – ADD RETAIL/BUILD SYSTEMS

R etail sales can be very powerful for your success and the success of your patients. This cost center has been proven to add up to $40,000.00 of additional recurring revenue each month for programs with a single surgeon or physician. Yes, that's up to $480,000 of additional revenue annually with a single physician program. This revenue will be higher with each additional physician or physician extender providing weight loss services in your practice. Quite frankly, having this additional cost center cushions inconsistencies with your operating revenue and supplements your income either way (while helping your patients succeed). It is also a great way to *profit share* between physicians and the hospital for hospital based programs as well.

I hate to be blunt, but if you are one of those people who say "Retail isn't for me or my patients", you need to get over it! Seriously! If your patients aren't buying quality protein products and vitamins from you, then they are buying sub-standard products from somewhere else. You owe it to yourself and to your patients to offer retail nutritional and vitamin products.

However, I want to make a distinction for you. You need to be providing them with physician prescribed protein products and pharmaceutical grade vitamins. You will be most successful if you sell items that they cannot obtain at local stores. Why? Because they are of a higher quality and you will be providing them with something unique. You cannot compete with the large vitamin store prices. They will always out price you (or else you will sell at a loss) because you cannot compete with their volume ordering which results in their lower wholesale cost and lower prices. What we have found is that the physician prescribed products also tend to taste better (if you do your homework) which puts you at an advantage over larger chain stores.

If your patients aren't buying quality protein products and vitamins from you, then they are buying sub-standard products from somewhere else.

I can confidently say that we can help just about any practice/health system set up a retail store and turn a profit almost immediately. Then, we help them keep their store profitable while growing it over time with monthly special ideas and marketing materials. This comes from experience selling the best quality, best tasting products and promoting them in a way that keeps patients happily coming back for more.

As a side note, a robust store generally does not occur by selecting one company that has protein products and signing a contract with them so you can only offer their products. It's not impossible, but a bit more challenging. Patients want and need more variety. In addition, some vendors have great tasting protein shakes and yet their protein bars have either too many carbohydrates or taste terrible. Other vendors may have wonderful snacks but nasty tasting protein shakes or soups. You need to taste test before you decide to sell the product.

If you are hesitant, let me take the pressure off. The joy in selling nutraceuticals in your office is that you (the physician) are NOT the salesperson. In fact, as a weight loss physician you will be prescribing a certain amount of protein to your patients along with certain vitamins. All you are doing with a retail store is making it convenient for patients to purchase those on the spot without YOU completing the sale. Even better, if done properly, it keeps them coming back and bringing their family and friends! This is a win-win for everyone.

> *The joy in selling nutraceuticals in your*
> *office is that you (the physician) are NOT*
> *the salesperson.*

Here's your step-by-step plan to build or enhance your retail store:

1. **Create your plan/budget for success:** Having an implementation plan and realistic budget with agreed upon minimal, target and stretch goals sets the stage for swift implementation. It also provides for an immediate return on investment (ROI) and lack of wasted time, resources and energy. Your goals will be dependent upon the size of your store and the number of practitioners.

You will also need to determine whether or not you are going to create an e-store for a greater reach and ease of ordering. A number of sales systems can accommodate both on-site and e-commerce as well. It is desirable to keep on-site and e-commerce sales in one system so that inventory can be maintained more efficiently. It is best to keep it simple at the beginning with just an on-site store but I mention e-commerce so that you can proactively ensure that it is a part of your software selection if e-commerce is included in your long-term plan.

Numbers are important. You should know what products have the highest sales, who your top buyers are (so you can reward them) and what products have the highest profit margin. It also helps to package some of your products together (i.e. vitamin pack) for higher sales and to offer a tempting discount for your patients.

Within your sales software, you will want to categorize each item you sell. I recommend leaving like items grouped together on your budget. However, you will still be able to drill down for each item within your sales software. For example, on your budget you might just have vitamins and nutritional products but in your sales system, you can actually look at each category such as shakes, bars, soups, snacks, entrees, and desserts. You can also look at sales by vendor. Your categories can grow as your store grows. It is important to note that if you plan to branch out into e-commerce, some software systems end up using these categories automatically to populate your online e-store. Thus, you will want to categorize them appropriately in a way customers would search for them online.

As for capital investment, you can begin by operating your store out of a closet. Thus, the only requirements would be sales software on one of your existing computers, a bar code reader (optional), shelving and your selected product. You can get my list of our favorite vendors at our website www.WeightLossPracticeBuilder.com/FreeResources. I place the resources online because they are updated frequently.

I recommend tracking your retail revenue/expenses as a separate cost center within your accounting software or this can be tracked as a totally separate business account depending upon ownership of the retail store and your preference. This is very important so you can track income, cost of goods sold, expenses and retail sales tax easily.

If you don't already have it, you will need to set up retail sales and use tax account with your state's government tax agency. Sales tax generally needs to be paid monthly and can usually be done easily online.

For some expenses that may be shared with your overhead office expenses, I recommend including them based upon the square footage of the store. For example, in one of our practices, the square footage is 10,000 feet and the store is 1,500 square feet. Thus, for telephone, rent and utilities, grounds maintenance and the like, they allocate 15% of the total monthly cost to the retail store. Salaries can be shared as well for this cost center depending upon the manpower needed for your particular size retail store.

Taking these things into consideration, a *basic* retail store budget outline might include:

Revenue:

- Vitamins
- Nutritional Products
- Other
- Shipping & Handling (for e-commerce only)

Total Income

Cost of Goods Sold (COGS):
- List each vendor you purchase products from to sell in your retail store

Total COGS

Gross Profit:

Total Revenue – COGS = Gross Profit

Expenses:
- Accounting
- Advertising & Promotion
- Bank Fees
- Credit Card Discount Fees
- CRM (Customer Relationship Marketing Software if you don't already have this in your current system)
- Event Supplies
- Grounds Maintenance
- Office Supplies

- Packaging Supplies
- Payroll
- Printing & Reproduction
- Rent
- Repairs & Maintenance
- Sales Operating Software
- Sales Tax Payable
- Shipping & Handling (for e-commerce)
- Telephone
- Uniforms (if applicable)
- Utilities
- Website

Total Expenses

Net Income:

Gross Profit – Expenses = Net Income

2. **Decide upon your timeframe for implementation:** Your retail store can be up and running in as little as 1 week depending upon how many products you desire to sell. If you are planning on a larger storefront, plan on 4-8 weeks. The timeframe is less as long as you follow a set plan as outlined here.

   Many vendors will private label your products. This means that they will send them to you with your logo on them. This is great for brand recognition. However, this is not usually possible until a certain volume of consistent ordering is established. This volume is different for each vendor. You do not need to get worried about this at the beginning and some choose not to private label at all.

As your store grows, I recommend private labeling as many items as you can as long as it won't result in too much product in your store that ends up as a loss when it becomes outdated and is disposed of instead of being sold. If you choose to private label, this will lengthen the timeframe for product delivery so you will need to take this into account as you determine the opening date for your retail store.

3. **Determine the right size store for your situation:** Your retail space can be as small as a closet or as large as our biggest storefront which is 1,500 square feet. In fact, you can begin operating from a closet and grow from there. This is also a great way to 'test the waters' if you are skeptical about having a retail store. Be careful though since skepticism by those in charge can prevent your store from ever getting off the ground. Trust me, you want a retail store. The benefits far outweigh any risks.

4. **Pick your products:** Product selection depends upon 4 things including: taste (for obvious reasons); nutritional content (that supports what your patients need); desire to private label (or not) and space (for storage requirements). Start small, see what sells best and then increase your par levels of stock.

A retail store may require a mindset change for you. For many clinicians (including myself), retail may feel "icky" or "salesy". As I mentioned previously, I can recommend tried and true vendors for you to evaluate at www.WeightLossPracticeBuilder.com/ FreeResources. Then, I recommend you obtain samples and have you and your staff complete a taste test. Once you find quality products you really like, it becomes very easy to promote them to your patients.

You can also experiment with various ways to prepare your nutritional supplements. For example, nearly everyone on our staff drinks a protein shake for breakfast. The one we use is delicious and starts our day out with 29 grams of protein and just 15 grams of carbs (the great 2:1 ratio you are likely familiar with). Some like to add their coffee to their shake as part of the water, others like to add an extract for a varied flavor and others like to add peanut butter protein powder (like me).

I recommend you let your staff purchase your protein products at cost. You want them to be very familiar with the products. In this way, promotion to patients becomes second nature. They are excited as they talk to the patients and sales happen with much less effort.

5. **Set up your sales systems:** Efficiency requires systemization. It also requires a natural balance of systemization with high customer service. You see your sales system is a combination of technology and personalized service.

When selecting your sales system, you can either integrate the product sales in your current computer system or integrate easy low cost solutions that also provide for an e-store and rewards programs for your patients to enjoy. The former is helpful for smaller stores and the latter positions you better for rapid growth. Neither is right or wrong, it just goes back to your overall goal(s).

It is not mandatory, but rewards programs can be set up in a variety of ways and truly boost sales. You can do something as simple as 10% off for every $100 spent or get a bit more savvy with a program that tracks all sales and offers money back depending upon the amount spent (even online). Or, you can integrate both! The sky is the limit and is only constrained by your imagination (and the imaginations of your awesome staff).

The bottom line is to have a system that is reliable and easy to use. It is helpful if an e-mail system is included (which is usually the case) along with e-commerce as I mentioned earlier. Your system should also track inventory. I have used systems that are totally manual to systems that have every bell and whistle you want. Make sure that it will support your current needs without adding significantly to your overhead and are able to grow with you over time. If you want to learn about some of my system recommendations, visit www. WeightLossPracticeBuilder.com/FreeResources or just e-mail me at Karol@WeightLossPracticeBuilder.com

6. **Train your staff:** Not only is technology training necessary but having a "cheerleader" who enjoys sales is extremely helpful. Customer service training is a great way to not only help your store sales, but increase patient referrals and the overall positive attitude/atmosphere throughout all service points of your program.

If you are hiring someone new to run your store and be your sales associate, I recommend hiring someone with an interest in heath/wellness but not a clinician or typical medical professional. I recommend hiring someone who loves sales and events. If you can get someone who is talented at creating graphics and sales materials as well, then that's an added bonus you will appreciate more than you know.

One of my greatest aha moments was when I was able to stop micro managing the retail store and let someone who loves sales take over. Our store manager is awesome. Surrounding yourself with great staff who understands your vision, are loyal, self-directed, happy and creative will exponentially increase the speed of your business growth and goal attainment. Then your job is to challenge them with new goals and be sure to treat them well.

I have always believed that if I can hire someone with excellent customer service and communication, I can teach them the rest. The interesting thing I have found is that if they have excellent customer service, they are usually also eager to learn new things and to do things right. These individuals are like a sponge and respond well to a positive example and are able to learn things quickly (especially if your operating systems are well documented).

I like to hire committed, self-directed employees and then challenge them with an outcome...not a task. They will likely rise to the occasion and come up with something spectacular in half the amount of time you would. I have more recommendations for effective practice management in chapter 13.

7. **Promote your products:** As I mentioned earlier, providing your staff (and yourself) with a cost effective way to use your retail products will help

them promote them to others. It's easy to promote your products when they believe in them and use them personally.

You can easily integrate promotion and education regarding your vitamins and supplements at office visits, in educational materials, via e-mail, text and/or social media. Having a promotional plan makes this easier and predictable so you never miss a beat...or sale!

It's easy to promote your products when you believe in them and use them personally.

Once you get up and running, you will want to create a monthly calendar that outlines your specials, new products and monthly events. You can do as little or as much as you want. Your calendar helps guide your posts and e-mails to your patients. Texts as well if you desire.

For example, in one month you may want to promote your B-Complex vitamins. That month you write a blog about energy and the effect these vitamins has on energy and weight loss. You then do a quick video (even on Facebook live) and post your blog and your video at different times on each of your social media channels. Your e-mail to patients includes a link to the blog and the video as well as specifics about the vitamin special. If you have an e-store, you can link directly to the product. Often you can have the option within your e-store software for them to indicate if they want it shipped or if they want to pick it up at your store (to avoid shipping). You have to make it simple! Once you get this up and running, you will actually be making sales while you sleep.

There are many more tactics with regards to this intellectual material you create that can significantly increase your online presence. With proper use of key words, you will also increase your organic search engine optimization. It's amazing what can happen once you get some momentum. Another beautiful aspect is that this is essentially free other than the time and effort you/your staff spend setting everything up and creating content. Your costs can increase if you utilize an outside source but even so the cost should not be significant. Your resulting ROI should be positive with the additional sales coming in.

8. **Track your positive ROI:** As I mentioned before, I recommend you track your retail store as a separate cost center. In this way, it is easier to track revenue, cost of goods sold, sales tax and any other associated costs. We recommend doing this at least monthly and specific to any promotions you offer (monitor those sales spikes). This will help you fine tune your strategies for rapid growth and marketing with a positive ROI.

If you find you are not experiencing a positive ROI (which is extremely rare), watch out for these common culprits:

- Improper allocation of corporate overhead to this cost center inflating expenses (more common with hospital programs)
- Poor product selection
- Lack of enthusiastic sales associates/employees

- Too many free giveaways
- Lack of coordinated promotion and follow-up
- Products not properly displayed
- Poor buy in from staff/practitioners
- Poor understanding of proper Par levels resulting in over-ordering

The great thing is that all of these culprits can be corrected for better product management and higher sales. After a period of three months, you should be able to better predict appropriate par levels and have your systems in place for proper marketing and sales. If you have one month with a poor ROI, address it immediately because this is not the norm.

9. **Implement growth strategies:** Once you have your retail store up and running, monitor what is working well, what needs fine tuning and what needs to be eliminated. Brainstorm growth strategies with your front line employees and be open to new "out of the box" ideas that make sense with your plan (see step 1).

Your retail store can be one of your most fun endeavors. It is also something you can incorporate for maximum promotion through your events and support groups. Coordinating patient education with your products will help sales and organic search engine optimization at the same time.

10

STEP 7 – GREAT PROCESS TO MARKET, MEASURE ROI AND GROW YOUR PRACTICE

The critical difference between programs that grow and those that stagnate or disappear altogether is that the growing program has a strategic marketing plan and is engaged with their prospective patients as well as their current patients. They have a relationship with them that naturally creates a buzz and additional patients coming through the door.

This chapter covers my GREAT process to promote your services, measure your return on investment (ROI) and grow your medical weight loss program. It also includes a few personal insights for maximizing your personal enjoyment of your practice.

Marketing is your strategy for promoting your program so you attract your ideal patients. This includes determining the best tactics for accomplishing your goal. Unfortunately, most people start with the tactics and throw out many broad messages through whatever medium (or bright shiny object) someone 'sold' them today.

Marketing is your <u>strategy</u> for promoting your program so you attract your ideal patients.

It is best to determine a simple marketing strategy that includes the right (specific) message to the right (specific) market delivered via the best medium (platform) where they commonly hang out or get their information. For example, promoting weight loss to your entire community may sound great – that way you can serve the greatest amount of people. But you would get better results if you focused your outcome driven message on a specific sub-set such as women who want to get back to their pre-baby weight or Type 2 diabetics who want to eliminate their medications and delivered it to them where they likely find their information (OB/GYN offices or Facebook for new moms and Physician offices or Facebook for diabetics).

If you have found a marketing specialist that is getting you great results in terms of attracting your ideal patients with a positive ROI and meeting/exceeding your goals, then I applaud you! That is not easy to do and you should stick with them.

More likely, you are not fully satisfied with your medical weight loss practice marketing efforts and want more. However, as a clinician, this is not what you were trained to do and quite possibly something you dislike doing. Nor do you have the time! In fact, the words marketing and sales may have negative connotations for you because they are often related to scams and being taken advantage of which never feels good.

However, helping people improve their health and do the things that bring them the most enjoyment feels great! Seeing someone with tears in their eyes as they step on the scale and hit their weight loss goal makes you smile yet tear up at the same time. Watching someone work out in your fitness class that could barely walk to their mailbox a few months ago makes you proud. This feeling never gets old.

So how do you bring in more patients with integrity and without feeling 'salesy'? How do you get your desired marketing results without having to do all of the work?

Marketing begins with your brand and your brand is more than your logo and color scheme. Your brand is the *relationship* you have with your patients. You are an integral part of this relationship as well as each and every one of your employees. You know your patients the best. You know their fears, pains, desires, what they love and what they hate. This is critically important to your marketing efforts.

Your brand is the relationship you have with your patients.

You see, people make choices and purchases based upon feelings. The experience that they have with you and your program is what creates their feelings – and what they will remember (and share with others).

When you think about creating a positive experience that helps your patients alleviate their fears, do more of what they love and less of what they dislike, it feels good. And yet, it's still marketing and sales. You are selling the experience. You know it is good for them and that it will impact them positively for a long time to come. That's the thing about weight loss services. It is a relationship and your patients don't forget you or what you/your staff have done for them. They are grateful forever.

> *People make choices based upon feelings*
> *created by their experience with you and*
> *your program – this is what they will*
> *remember and share with others.*

Unfortunately, we had a hard time finding an effective marketing company and were tired of spending a lot of money with little or no return on our investment. We abide by the mantra you can do anything you set your mind to so we chose to learn (a lot) and create our own strategies to connect with our ideal patients. We actually operate our entire marketing program in house through our staff that knows our patients best. As I have mentioned before, you might be surprised what hidden talents your staff has if you ask and give them the chance to grow. This has proven to be wildly successful and much less costly for us.

So it's time to share with you not only what works, but works very well when it comes to effectively marketing medical weight loss programs. This means attracting your ideal patients, creating positive relationships, growing your program and having fun along the way.

I could spend a lot of time on marketing fundamentals but I know what you are most interested in are the steps that will get you to faster success along with specific tactics you can implement right away.

***You might be surprised what hidden talents
your staff has if you ask and give them the
chance to grow.***

Thus, after a lot of study and decades of practical application, I am going to share with you a simple big picture and then 6 steps that will serve as a laser focused guide for you and your team. As a big picture in the lifecycle of getting more patients, *you want 4 things to happen.* They include:

1. Attract your ideal customers/patients
2. Build a quality relationship with them
3. Convert them to a weight loss program or other services as appropriate
4. Turn these patients into Raving Fans that send more patients your way

In order to make these 4 things happen, you will want to follow something called a GREAT process for marketing success. I tried to make it only 3 steps but in reality, it is 6 important steps. As I mentioned earlier, most people like to start at Step 5 since when you are fulfilling tactics, you are *doing* something. However, the reality is that Step 5 will be somewhat worthless (or random) and can cause you to waste a fair amount of time and money if performed prior to completing Steps 1-4. You see planning (even if you think it is boring) will save you immense amounts of time and frustration. Like most of you, I like a fun adventure that doesn't include a map but not when I need to be efficient and I am determined to obtain a specific result. Just trust me; you need to do these in order. And I also included a case study at the end so you can see the plan in action.

Karol's GREAT Process for Weight Loss Program Marketing Success

1. **Goal:** Determine Your Goal/Desired Outcome
2. **Rare:** Verify What Makes You a Rare Gem/ Unique
3. **Emotional Triggers:** Identify the Primary Pain Points of Your Ideal Patient/Client (your Avatar)
4. **Approach:** Map out Your Strategy (Right Market/Right Message/Right Media)
5. **Tactics:** Create Your Actionable Calendar & Implement Appropriate Tactics (most people mistakenly start here)
6. **Test:** Measure, Refine, Re-Deploy

Step 1: Goal: Determine Your Goal/Desired Outcome:

So what is it you want to accomplish? And don't think too small. Where do you want to grow? Do you want more patients? Do you want more retail revenue? Do you want to implement a new weight loss program? Do you want more referrals? What is it? The key here is to keep it simple and make it measurable.

Depending upon the size of your organization and your team, you may have more than one goal. But I caution you to keep it simple and work towards some great wins before you get too greedy with the process.

Have you heard of the *12 Week Year?*[12] It's a book well worth reading and a system that improves your ability to get things done. The underlying premise is that the one thing holding you back from achieving more in your life is execution. You don't do the work necessary to make your goals happen. In the 12 Week Year, instead of thinking of your goals in terms of 12 months, you fulfill your goals in 12 weeks and move on to the next. One of the great things about that with regards to your marketing plan is that it keeps you moving, keeps you accountable (you only have 12 weeks right?) and if your marketing strategy was an online evergreen one (almost like being on auto pilot), you are on to your next strategy while your previous one is still working for you! It's wonderful.

Bottom line for this step is to identify your desired outcome. When you do, be sure that it is simple and measurable.

Step 2: Rare: Verify What Makes You a Rare Gem/ Unique

When I say "you", of course I mean what makes you and your program stand out in a crowd? What would make a person choose you over other programs or products available to them? It's a question you might not think about often. I mean it's considered arrogant to tout your talents around town isn't it? However, when you have a crowded market and competitors across the street or across town or on many TV commercials, you need to figure out what makes you unique. Why do your patients choose you and your program?

You need to know this because you will use it as a way to attract patients. You will understand this better as we dig deeper into these steps. In fact, if you used it as a message such as "Come to Program X because we are the best." that wouldn't work. It could be viewed as arrogant and annoying. People want to know *why* you are the best.

A better way to use your strengths is as a complement to the problems and fears that your potential patients may have. For example, if they are fearful of failure, knowing you have the an 85% success rate for weight loss even 1 year after initial success would be helpful. Or if your potential patients want convenience, it would be great for them to know that you offer a 'one stop shop' and can accommodate online education and convenient appointment scheduling. Knowing your unique competitive advantage is important and will be paired with what you identify in Step 3. This is very different from just saying we are the best or we are the most experienced without linking it to why that would be important to the patient and what 'pain' you are able to solve for them.

Step 3: Emotional Triggers: Identify the Primary Pain Points of Your ideal Patient (Your Avatar)

Now you and your team need to brainstorm your ideal customer or avatar. And you know, it shouldn't be 'everyone'. Think about them and define the following (be specific). As you do this, put in your mind a picture of a patient you really, really enjoy working with. Define these aspects as if you are describing them and then broaden it some as desired.

- Age range
- Gender
- Occupation
- Income Level
- Educational Level
- Geographic Location
- Co-morbidities
- Specialists they go to
- Insurance Type (if applicable)

Once you have defined your ideal patient, think about what their main problems, challenges and pain points (what's really bothering them that caused them to come see you for treatment). You will want to know that because in your marketing message, you are going to want to agitate that problem just a bit so that you can adequately catch their attention. This may seem silly to you but it is very important to be very specific. You are going to create your marketing message as if you are speaking *directly* to that patient you were thinking of that you enjoy working with.

Once you come up with a long list, separate out what you feel are the top 5 pain points. These will be helpful as you develop your content and marketing plan.

Step 4: Approach: Map Out Your Strategy (Right Market/Right Message/Right Media)

This sounds involved but it is fairly straight forward. This is where you will create your strategy for reaching the ideal client you identified above. This is your *right market.* If you know your outcome/goal and who it is that you are trying to reach, that's half the battle.

After that, it is time to determine the *right message.* For this, you will combine one of their top pain points to what it is that you are offering. In your message, you want to catch their attention in an authentic, sincere and ethical way. This is the time to get your team together and brainstorm. If you are promoting weight loss surgery and one of your staff has had the procedure, they would be a great reality check as to whether or not your message resonates.

For clinicians, the marketing message is what may feel uncomfortable. However, if you tie it to an educational blog or video (something you talk about or teach every day), it makes more sense and is perceived as more valuable to the patient. You can see a great example of this in the case study presented shortly. Connecting your message to a primary pain point (diabetes, high cost of medications, inability to be as active as they desire, joint pain) and messaging how you and your services can help solve this problem will be most compelling. Communicating this message through a patient testimonial can be very compelling.

If you follow this method, then what you are actually creating is something called a "lead magnet" which is something that is perceived to be valuable to your ideal customer (and great information they need). It is something that they are willing to exchange their name and e-mail or other contact information in order to obtain it. Once you have that, you can continue to nurture your relationship with additional helpful information and at some point, if they make the decision to pursue treatment, you will likely be the one they will choose. You will be top of mind.

Finally, you must determine the *right media.* You can choose one type of media or test your message through a number of media sources. Some choices are listed below. The more you test your media channels, the more you will understand which are your most successful and which you can avoid at this time.

Your media choice will be dependent upon where your ideal patient 'hangs out'. Depending upon the demographic you identified, they could get their information through traditional marketing (i.e. brochures, direct sales, TV, radio, printed advertisements, and direct mail). Another type of marketing source is on the internet (i.e. e-mail campaign, social media, blogs, podcasts and resulting search engine optimization). For healthcare, another source is direct referral from their physician(s) and if you are a primary care physician, your market is already at your fingertips.

For referrals from other physicians, you actually market to the healthcare provider directly. They are usually interested in your outcome data and ease of referral to your center. In addition, they desire a positive patient experience and communication regarding the patient. Nurturing these relationships tends to be very time consuming and somewhat frustrating because you have to get by the 'gatekeeper' at the front desk. Nonetheless, these efforts can be very worthwhile.

Step 5: Tactics: Create Your Actionable Calendar & Implement Appropriate Tactics (most people mistakenly start here)

Here is where people get excited. You have your ideal patient identified, you know where they hang out, and you have created your message that identifies their pain point and why your service or product is their solution. Now it is time to create your actionable calendar. This identifies specific plans for creating your marketing ad, details about printing or online ad approval/placement, who has responsibility for each action, what is being posted where and when (day/time). It is all in front of you so you and your team are crystal clear as to when the campaign is going to run, what the budget is and how to measure the outcome. Now is the time to clarify questions and then deploy the plan.

Here are a few tips for the Tactic step in the GREAT process:

- Start Small (it can be very time consuming)
- Consider Your Internal vs. External Resources/ Assets so you might not have to start from scratch
- Set Up Your Schedule and Stick to It
- Automate Social Media Posts When Possible (saves time & energy)
- Don't Schedule Too Far In Advance – Trends Change
- Be Ready to Respond to a Trend in Your Area of Expertise

- Use Graphics/Video (be wary of copyright laws and have signed release from clients on file)
- Each Post Should Have a Clear Call to Action (CTA) so the patient knows exactly what to do or where to call

Step 6: Test: Measure, Refine, Re-Deploy

Keeping track of your analytics can help determine if you are spending your time and efforts in the right way. From a financial perspective, your return on investment (ROI) should be at least a 3:1 ratio (if $500 was spent your return should be $1,500 or more). You can track your analytics in a variety of ways:

- Google Analytics
- Facebook Analytics
- Internal statistics
- Other lead generation software if you use them for lead capture such as Leadpages, Active Campaign, Kajabi or Clickfunnels to name a few.

Once you determine your ROI, it is time to determine if you just need to tweak your ad, do some split testing or re-deploy an entirely different ad. Usually it is a matter of tweaking your ad message, where your message is being deployed or the specific market where you chose to send it. Thus, you want to look at your market, message and media source(s) and make changes as necessary.

Case Study: Bariatric Surgery Program

Step 1: Goal: Increase number of cases/month/ surgeon to 30

Step 2: Rare/Unique Characteristics

- Most experienced surgeons in the region
- Good Reputation
- Best-Selling Author

Step 3: Emotional Triggers

- Fear of surgery
- Poor health/co-morbidities
- Not feeling 'normal' and fitting in/being able to do everyday activities
- Joint pain
- Lack of energy

Step 4: Approach

- Right market: men/women who need to lose 75+ pounds, are interested in surgery but have a lot of questions, educated, professional, committed to change
- Right message: Is weight loss surgery right for you? Get your free book from best-selling author and the regions most experienced weight loss surgeon. Sign up here or call (999) 999-9999

- Right media: Facebook ad for people who met the demographic above and lived in the same state as the program

Step 5: Tactics

- The ad was created and deployed as a Facebook campaign for the identified audience. Re-targeting pixels were set in place and an ad buy for a maximum spend of $25/day for 30 days was put into place.

Step 6: Test

- Measure/Refine/Re-Deploy: It took 3 tries to get the ad approved on Facebook which is common with nearly all weight loss ads. Once approved, the ad spend the first month was $540. The campaign resulted in 30 books being requested/downloaded. All were put into an e-mail sequence. 4 people have contacted the office and scheduled 1:1 visits with the physician. Two are insurance and two are potential self-pay surgeries. One self-pay followed through thus far with surgery resulting in a 9:1 ROI

- While the ROI is great, this is not meeting the initial objective. Thus, we will refine the ad with split testing 2 different ad messages and review our follow-through for interested patients

- In the meantime, with the great 9:1 ROI, the current ad will continue!

To be a sustainable business, you must be able to create messages that matches the wants/needs of your ideal client.

As a summary, some of the most helpful marketing tactics for weight loss programs and their retail stores include:

- Platform/Brand/Relationships
- Online Webinars
- Organic Search (website, keywords, optimization)
- Targeted e-Mail Marketing (sales & educational)
- Text Messaging
- Physician Referrals
- Testimonials (written/video)
- Engaging Social Media Posts with Editorial Calendar for ease of implementation – Facebook, Pinterest, You Tube, Twitter
- Best-Selling Author/Books
- Facebook Campaigns/Lead Magnets/Sales Funnel
- Facebook Live
- Onsite Electronic Sign
- Optimized Rich Content (video, audio, written)
- Building Our Ubiquity Footprint Over Time
- Weight Management University for Weight Loss Surgery™ turnkey educational program
- Clear Branding

- Other Helpful Options:
  - o Radio/Expert Presentations/Interviews
  - o Medical Tourism
  - o Podcasts
  - o Fliers
  - o Referral Program
  - o Cross-Selling
  - o Posters
  - o Radio/TV Personality Having Surgery
  - o Donations
  - o Letting local organizations utilize our space (foot traffic)

You don't need to introduce all of these tactics to your plan. You just need to implement the ones that interest you the most and that you feel will get the right message, to the right market (people) via the right media option. In fact, if you try to do too many tactics at once, you will feel frustrated, overwhelmed and financially drained (and drive your team crazy).

As promised, below are some of my personal insights that can significantly increase the overall enjoyment of your medical weight loss program and life in general:

Have a Passion for What You Do

There is no denying the fact that if you love what you do, you are happier and much more effective. It doesn't even feel like 'work'. Rather your passion creates joy, motivation and positive outcomes with faster results. This may sound a little surreal or unrealistic but it is so true! You can't fake passion. When you are passionate, your actions are much more believable and inspirational. This is especially true when it comes to building a successful weight loss practice.

Let's face it, weight loss is hard! So having a practitioner that is passionate about helping others lose weight and improve their health is very important. If it's not you, don't stress it – the passion can also come from your physician extenders and staff. This passion (and overall vibe) will differentiate you from others who may be building a weight loss business for the wrong reasons.

Practice What You Preach

It is easiest to coach people to success when you are successful yourself. It also feels congruent when your personal values match your professional values and goals. This can bring extreme enjoyment and peace. I am not saying you need to be perfect or even close to perfect, but I am saying that you should try to walk the talk and practice what you preach.

You wouldn't seek financial advice from a company that just went bankrupt just as you wouldn't likely seek health advice from someone who isn't somewhat healthy themselves. There is the thought that misery loves company and if your practitioner is "in the same boat" they will better understand, but that's not the way to the path of improvement.

Similarly, in any sport, it is better to play with those more skilled than you – that's how your game improves and how you challenge yourself to get to the next level. Another natural outcome is that your level of accountability for your own health usually becomes more intense when you are providing weight loss services. As a result, you are healthier, happier, driven and more creative. When you feel your best, you tend to bring out the best in others. Positivity and great results are contagious!

Be Intentional

We are creatures of habit and usually don't like change. So often you may go about your day doing the same things even though your actions aren't creating the outcome you desire. You may feel stuck and simply used to doing things the way you always did them. And frankly, that feels comfortable and safe.

You also are extremely busy or overwhelmed and taking time to really think about what you want personally and professionally isn't possible with your schedule. Or so you believe...

No one can do this for you but it is critical to your success and happiness. If you don't know where you are going, you can't be intentional about your day to day activities and before you know it, years have passed by and you just continue to be in the same rut. And one day, you may regret not pursuing what you really want and deserve.

Believe me, I fought this for a long time and wouldn't have succeeded in building a number of successful businesses unless I got over my fears and reasons for procrastination. I also worked with a coach to help me break out of my rut and create my vision. In addition, I shared this with my husband. He is a great sounding board and helps to support my vision/actions. This method also works for our children as well. We like to break it down this way:

1. 3 Year Vision – My 'Why' or motivation. I describe exactly what my life will look like in 3 years from a personal and professional perspective. I write this in present tense as if it is 3 years from now.

2. 1 Year Goals – My 'What' I have accomplished over the next year. I write this in present tense as if it is one year from now.

3. 90 Day Strategy – My 'How' to accomplish my goals. I list my 'Top 3 Projects' along with the most important 4-8 actions that will get me where I want to go.

4. This Week's Actions – My 'Now' actions that relate to my 90 day strategy. I revise this weekly and then make sure the actions are incorporated into my daily schedule that week.

I document this in one table with 4 boxes and keep it in front of me each day to keep me focused and 'Intentional'. This is key for me because if my actions are intentional (deliberate, conscious, done on purpose), I see progress. Otherwise, I let others drive my schedule by constantly volunteering, putting fires out and being 'busy' instead of accomplishing my weekly actions...which contribute to my top 3 projects...which lead me to attaining my goals...and living the life I envision and desire.

Don't Be Afraid to Add a Retail Store

I used to think retail felt a bit weird. We are healthcare providers and the thought of sales felt terrible. We dabbled with a very small store (literally in a closet) and soon I realized that the products we carefully selected actually improved patient outcomes. I discovered that they loved having products available to them and that our retail store helps to build a stronger relationship since it keeps them coming back. Believe it or not, our retail store generates $480,000+ gross revenue each year.

And, once you have a wonderful retail manager (again surrounding yourself with great people) with systems in place you don't have to be the salesperson. Retail doesn't have to feel salesy. You are actually helping your patients get better results and adding another revenue stream into your practice.

Learn from Your Experiences (success & failures alike)

Just like long term weight loss, business success and life is a journey that is experienced minute to minute and day to day. We need to take it one day at a time and learn to enjoy it more.

In your program, you will experience success and failures. These lay the foundation for positive growth – if you let them. We view failures as a learning experience and then we move on. I encourage you to do the same.

Learning from your past can be hard to do. You may think your past defines who you are today. The reality is that your past does not predict your future. Only you have control over your destiny.

11

THE SIMPLEST, MOST COST EFFECTIVE WAY TO GET STARTED

There is no doubt that starting your medical weight loss program from scratch is extremely rewarding. However, it will definitely take a fair amount of time and effort which many busy physicians simply don't have. That's why I find many physicians opt for implementing a medical weight loss program that has been proven successful for patients, profitable for practices and maps out exactly what to do in order to be up and running as quickly as possible.

If you go to any of the national weight loss conferences, you will find some vendors there promoting their medical weight loss program. Most of them are nutraceutical companies that focus their programs around their products. Some are very well put together and also include training and marketing materials along with guidelines for not only their products but how to help your patient's transition to regular natural food products. In fact, I have great relationships with many of these corporations and integrate their products into physician based nutritional retail stores for the offices I consult with. I do not recommend a medical weight loss program contract only with one company in order to run their program due to lack of variety and access to other companies with great tasting products with competitive pricing.

In addition, there are some multi-level nutritional product based companies that target physicians desiring to add weight loss products into their practice. I have not found one as of yet that I am comfortable recommending.

To be completely transparent (if you didn't notice already), at Weight Loss Practice Builder, we have created a medical weight loss program that can be implemented into any practice as well. It includes flexible, low cost licensing of a comprehensive medical weight loss program called My Weight Loss Academy™ which was created by a board certified bariatrician. The program can be implemented into your office in a variety of ways:

1. The physician/practice simply sells patients access to the online My Weight Loss Academy™ program. The practice can charge patients whatever they desire for their access to the program or bundle it with current services as desired. The implementation of this online medical weight loss program includes:

   • Creation of customized promotional materials for program promotion (flier, social media graphic)

   • Creation of unique practice site/url for patient access to My Weight Loss Academy program and bonus materials for their patients

- Unlimited patient access to My Weight Loss Academy online program along with current e-mail sequence for automated delivery of program to patient inbox.
- Monthly patient membership site maintenance and patient assistance as necessary.
- Counselor/coach access to program.

2. The physician/practice not only offers the online program as outlined above but also provides counseling in their office to complement the program and add accountability. In addition to revenue they collect for the program, the practice also charges whatever they desire for these counseling/coaching visits or charges through patient insurance as an office visit with their practitioner. The implementation of this option includes everything in #1 above as well as:

- Training for counselor(s) including what to cover at each visit, orientation to program and templated clinician documentation forms that accompany program
- Ongoing training as necessary including weekly/ monthly implementation video training calls.
- Monthly patient tip sheets/recipes customized to practice for additional patient education as desired.

Optional:

- Customization (white labeling) of educational materials with practice logo and physician bio for PDF course downloads, e-mail sequences for program launch and accompanying course video personalized intro as if the practitioner created them themselves.

- Marketing plan for practice to implement for optimal promotion of program.

Optional:

- Add easy to sell retail services to include Jump Start and Mini Jump Start Programs (product purchased by practice separately):
  - ✓ Creation of customized promotional materials and patient guides.
  - ✓ 3 Coaching calls for proper ordering of supplements and optimal quick implementation of program

Your profits are unlimited based upon what you charge for the program and how many you sell. The addition of counseling services enhances patient results and provides you or your extender with the necessary training to offer weight loss services in your office as cash pay services or billed through patient insurance which adds to the program revenue. Adding the Jump start programs provides you with one more revenue stream without having to implement a full retail store. The patient educational materials for the jump start programs are customized to your practice for easy sales.

An example of your promotional sales sheet is below:

Your Logo Here

Created by Center for Weight Loss Success

The 6-Month Simplified Weight Loss Program You can Live with for Life!

My Weight Loss Academy™ is an online program that simplifies what you need to know so you not only lose weight but understand how to keep it off for life! Over the past two decades, Dr. Thomas W. Clark has dedicated his career to helping thousands of people lose weight by turning complex weight loss information into easy-to-implement actions. You now have the ability to finally experience long-term successful weight loss, feel better, have more energy, live an active life and focus on what you "can" do rather than what you "can't" do. This will realize you have been making weight loss more complicated (and less fun) than it has to be.

Program includes:

My Weight Loss Academy™ digital program.
Includes immediate access to 14 modules of training (written material, videos & PDF action guides) conveniently available via your online membership site (access to all materials available for 7 months) and downloadable for continued use). You can move at your own pace or follow the step-by-step program instructions you will receive each week/month via e-mail for accountability and easy to follow guidance. See reverse side for details.

BONUS 21 Day Challenge. Your Weight Loss Plan for a Lifetime of Success!
Change Your Habits. Change Your Life—one day at a time. This easy to follow, day by day guide shows you how. Accept the challenge and feel the difference!

BONUS 6-month Losing Weight USA membership.
Puts you on the fast track to quicker results and provides direct access to one of the most experienced bariatric surgeons and bariatricians in the United States. Dr. Clark's weekly live weekly live webinars cover topics filled with information on how to increase your weight loss efforts. Be ready with your questions. He has answers! Each week also brings you new tip sheets, recipes and fitness ideas. Visit www.losingweightusa.com for full details.

BONUS Easy to Use Meal Planning & Journaling Templates (PDF)

BONUS Online Healthy Recipe Book (PDF)

BONUS Carbohydrate Counter Tool (PDF) Remove the mystery of counting carbs!

BONUS Weekly Lifestyle & Behavior Modification "How To" Classes
Learn not only what to do, but more importantly how to do it with these proven strategies

You determine the price

www.YourWebpageURL.com

Your Name and webpage url HERE

Your Address, Phone, Email and Website info HERE

If this turn-key program is something you are interested in learning more about, please contact the author at Karol@ WeightLossPracticeBuilder.com or schedule directly at www.smarturl.it/bookkarol. We can also brainstorm your ideas for creating your own program or a more robust retail store if that is your desire.

In addition to the modules below and the many bonuses already included, your membership site is filled with fitness tips/videos, tasty recipes and inspiration to keep you motivated. Your weight loss success at your fingertips!

My Weight Loss ACADEMY

Core Modules	Includes 14 Chapters, Videos and Accompanying Action Guides (PDF)
Making the Most of Your Program	Welcome to My Weight Loss Academy™. Dr. Clark shows you how the program works and tips for how to make the most of your "last" weight loss program for results that will last.
1. Getting Started	Motivation happens with quick results. This module shows you how to maximize your investment with quick implementation and weight loss to keep you going. Learn what you can begin today and the top thing you need to focus on – so need to feel overwhelmed.
2. Accountability	Setting up an accountability plan keeps you on track now and over time is critical to your success. This module shows you how without overwhelming you.
3. How to Get Results	Arguably the most important module in this program. You will learn how to do the simple math to determine your optimal eating plan. You will also learn the difference between "eating healthy" and "eating healthy to lose weight". Weight loss doesn't have to be complicated. Eating healthy made easy for you!
4. What Counts & What to Count?	This module teaches you what really counts when it comes to what you are eating. You will learn what you need to count for optimal success without overwhelming you with unnecessary tracking you don't need to worry about. Includes your 1, 2, 3 plan that simplifies not only what you need to eat but how to stay satisfied.
5. Vitamin & Meal Replacements	No need for confusion when it comes to the many vitamins and supplements available. This module clarifies what you need for optimal results. You will look and feel your best!
6. Fitness that Works for You	Fitness that begins at your level. This module teaches you what you may not know about exercise and how to make it an enjoyable part of your routine.
7. Eating In/Eating Out	This module makes eating in and eating out a breeze. You will learn how to make your healthy choices with ease – no need to stress here!
8. Carbohydrates	The good, the bad and the ugly is simplified for you when it comes to eating carbohydrates. This module includes the information you must know for best results.
9. Stress...less	Stress – we all have it. You will learn how stress affects your body and your ability to lose weight. It also shows you the best ways to conquer your stress!
10. Protein	Protein is a misunderstood macronutrient. This module gives you the skinny on protein, staying satisfied and building the metabolism you desire.
11. The Most Important Exercise	You will finally learn the fitness side of building your ideal metabolism – for weight loss and long term weight management. Don't miss this one!
12. What about Fat?	Fat is another very misunderstood macronutrient. You don't have to live in fear – learn what you do and don't want to eat when it comes to fat choices. Fat isn't necessarily making you fat!
13. How to conquer your saboteurs!	Saboteurs seem to be everywhere...especially if the saboteur is you! This module provides you with concrete advice on how to not only identify the saboteur people/situations in your life but how to overcome this negativity that can (and will) prevent you from your ultimate success as well.
14. Where do I go from here?	You have lost weight, your blood sugar is under control, your activity has improved (and you actually look forward to it), your lean body mass is higher – don't lose your momentum – this module continues your plan for long-term success. No more yo-yo dieting for you!

Your Address, Phone, Email and Website Info HERE

BONUS CHAPTERS

ADAPTED IN PART FROM
#1 BEST-SELLING BOOK

---

5 Profit Engines of a Successful Bariatric Surgery Practice: Your Blueprint for Building an Enjoyable Business that Creates Healthy Patients and a Healthy Bottom Line

12

SOCIAL MEDIA THAT SUPPORTS YOUR
PRACTICE AND YOUR PATIENTS

Social media is a great way to promote your business, provide engagement and create more buzz. Using social media to create more buzz is something recommended for nearly all businesses – including your weight loss practice. Think about it. People are 'connected' nearly all of their waking hours. Some people actually look at their phone just prior to bed and first thing when they wake up – even before they brush their teeth.

Never before has it been easier to be close to your ideal customers/patients. However, it is also very noisy out there and it is difficult to get and keep their attention. This is where (as I have mentioned throughout the book) it is critical for you to understand who your ideal patient is, what their pain points are (what keeps them up at night) and where they hang out.

You can build your relationship through quality content and positive posts. In fact, I recommend 6 informational posts to every 1 promotional post about your products or services. If you are viewed as the salesy one, it can be a total turn off and actually drive potential patients away.

I get asked frequently to set up and manage various business social media posts, online campaigns and e-mail marketing systems for clients. In fact, I could have a very lucrative business doing so and many national companies do just that. However, I believe that you shouldn't leave your online reputation to someone else. My team and I would rather teach you how to do it and provide you with quality monthly content and campaign ideas as desired so you ultimately have control over what is posted and when.

You will drive yourself crazy if you try to learn every social media platform at the same time. So don't do it! However, as you advance, you can get more of a bang for your buck by creating a post and then getting it out there on multiple platforms at the same time. In fact, there are some great services such as HootSuite (www.hootsuite.com), IFTT (www.iftt.com) or Meet Edgar (www.MeetEdgar.com) that will take your single post and distribute it across all of your social networking sites.

> *You will drive yourself crazy if you try to learn every social media platform at the same time.*

There are other social media platforms such as Snapchat, Vine, Tumblr and Yelp. However, I have found that the top platforms for weight loss practices include:

- Facebook (https://www.facebook.com) is the largest social site with over 2 billion users. This platform is familiar to most (especially males and females ages 35-54) and is used for socializing and building relationships (sound familiar?). People use Facebook to connect with others, to expose their brand and create customer engagement.

- Instagram (http://www.instagram.com) is primarily an image sharing platform for pictures and short videos. At the time this book was published, it was estimated that there are 800 million users on Instagram. This platform used to be dominated by teens but now attracts people in their 20's, 30's, 40's and beyond. Popularity for businesses continues to grow and studies have shown that 80% of Instagram users voluntarily connect with a brand.

- YouTube (http://youtube.com) If you want to see how popular YouTube can be for your practice visit www.youtube.com/docweightloss and you will see it in action for a robust bariatric surgery practice. YouTube is an online video hosting service. Some people don't think of it as a social networking site but with the ability to easily share videos and make comments (along with adding keywords for effective searches); this platform makes it very powerful for building your brand and sharing your knowledge. YouTube can also be set up to automatically feed to Twitter and Google+.

- Pinterest (http://pinterest.com) is dominated by women but likely your practice is dominated by women as well. This platform has been surprisingly effective at bringing in patients to many weight loss practices. This platform is all about images, especially photos and infographics. It has been shown that Pinterest users spend the most amount of money of any of the social media channels. This is a great place to share healthy recipes as well. Pinterest is where many of our website backlinks come from.

- Blogs (https://www.blogger.com or http://www. wordpress.org for free or self-hosted http://www. wordpress.com) are very popular for content sharing. In fact at least 25% of internet time is spent on blogs and social networks. Companies with blogs have many more inbound links than those without blogs which can help with organic SEO. One of the things I love about blogs is that you can write the blog and then easily share it on your other social media platforms for additional links back to your site. You can do a standard written blog or use video, sometimes called a vlog. Below is a representation of what I mean.

- Twitter (http://www.twitter.com) is great for instant news and shorter conversations. Quite frankly, I have not seen this to be very helpful for weight loss physicians other than to connect to other professionals, try to drive traffic to your website or to promote an online live event. Tweets have a short life so you need to repeat tweets to be most effective. However, Twitter does have your ideal demographic hanging out there – 65% females and typically 25-54 years of age. Twitter can be set up to automatically feed to Facebook or vice versa.

- LinkedIn (http://www.linkedin.com) is not only for getting your resume out there. It is known as the corporate, professional or employee site for social media. It is a professional site and I feel it is best utilized for business to business activities and interacting in professional groups of interest to you. Thus, not necessarily for obtaining new weight loss patients.

- Google+ (http://googleplus.com) has grown in popularity. It is a social networking site offered by Google. It provides you with a way to do free video and communicate with one person or groups of people. Their primary audience is 18-34 year olds.

My top three choices if you are just starting out would be your Blog, Facebook and Pinterest. Each post you make should be created with your ideal patient in mind. Think about the topics they ask you the most questions about and begin there. To make it really easy for you, just answer those top questions in a blog post, share that to your Facebook page, make a great graphic that goes along with it and post on Pinterest. And by the way, if you have no idea how to create graphics, there are great programs out there for you to use. At the moment, my team and I like to use Canva, YouZign and Publisher.

You might be used to random posts because that's all you have time for. This may be easier but your results will improve if you actually schedule what you will post about (message), where you will post it (media), to whom you are trying to attract (market) and when (calendar). As discussed earlier, this is where your editorial calendar will come in handy to bring it all together. We prepare ours on a simple spreadsheet but if you search Social Media Calendars, you will find a plethora of ideas and examples. While writing this book, I did a search and found this resource quite helpful https://blog.hootsuite.com/how-to-create-a-social-media-content-calendar/ Remember to also stay in touch with the latest general and weight loss news so you can modify your posts as necessary and maximize your relevant impact.

For our clients that use online marketing effectively, they are finding on average 30% of their referrals find them organically online. This is amazing - You are getting new referrals as well as building your organic SEO rankings all at the same time. Now that's a beautiful thing!

As with any resource such as what I have provided here, none of it matters if you don't implement! And don't think it has to be perfect. Yes, your reputation is of utmost concern but social media is intended to be conversational. Creativity pays off here. You can get going in a few simple steps:

1. Decide which social media platforms you want to use and sign up for your free accounts.
2. Decide who is going to manage your posts.
3. Create your editorial calendar.
4. Implement your plan!

You are educating first and then promoting your services at about a 6:1 ratio. When it comes time for your promotion, you will want to be sure to have a clear call to action (CTA). Most social media platforms make it easy for you to offer your CTA which is where you will either have a lead magnet valuable enough for the person to enter their name and e-mail or you may be linking directly to an online educational product or a product from your retail store. The bottom line is to make sure your CTA doesn't get lost. You should only ask them to do one thing and then make that one thing super easy to do.

For example, if you offered a 1 page infographic on the benefits of weight loss and you want people to give you their name and e-mail prior to download, you don't want to take them to your main website page that is filled with a lot of other information. Rather you want to take them to a clean, professional landing page that has just one thing to do – show what they get and include a place near the top of the page for them to enter their information. Then they automatically see a simple thank you page and the resource is downloadable from that page or sent to their e-mail. I prefer e-mail because then they can confirm their e-mail (required) so you know they agree to future nurturing e-mails you will send. As you might have guessed, these future e-mails will include more valuable information you know they want/need and eventually information about your services in the event they are interested in making a purchase and guide them to your main website.

You can make social media as hard or as easy as you want. You won't know until you try. I believe that if you follow these simple instructions, you will be glad you took the plunge.

A word of caution: When creating graphics, only use your own photos (with permission if it includes patients) or royalty free photos. This is mandatory in order to keep you out of trouble. No larger corporation who monitors use of photos on the internet cares if you "accidentally" used the photo without permission or "didn't know". They will take legal action usually in the form of a fine and this is something you must avoid.

13

KEYS TO EFFECTIVE PRACTICE MANAGEMENT

We have a sign in the reception area that simply states "Happy to Be Here". I smile every time I see it because I am happy to be here. If I wasn't, it would be time to make a change.

Fortunately, I think most of the team feels that way because we have a negligible staff turnover rate unless someone moves or are adversely affecting the operations of the office and/or quality of patient care.

Your office tends to have a 'vibe' (sometimes more officially referred to as your culture) that can be perceived by just about anyone who enters your office. Your 'vibe' begins at the top of your organization but can be influenced positively or negatively at any level. Remember earlier when you read that people buy based upon their feelings? Well your vibe is the feeling of your place of business. So it's important to pay attention to it.

What kind of vibe do you desire? Have you ever thought about it? If you haven't, I recommend you do. Especially if you are in a leadership position because you influence others perhaps more than you realize.

In our case, we enjoy a positive vibe that promotes respect, problem solving, teamwork, independent thoughts/ideas, creativity, caring, loyalty and determination to be your best. Now that's a lot!

I am not saying we are perfect at attaining all of these actions and have a perfect vibe each and every day, but it is something we strive towards. It is also an expectation for everyone no matter what position they hold. So how do you create such a seemingly elusive workplace vibe such as this? It is created by the people who work there and their relationships with each other and the customer (patient in this case). It is influenced by 3 things and I will break each of them down:

Influencers of Your Business Vibe

- Your Team
- Your Operations
- Your Wow Factor

Your Team

Your team is your greatest asset. You can have the most beautiful building in town, more money than you need, the most reputable physician or the best location around but if your team stinks (and I think you know what I mean), your overall success and reputation will suffer.

After effectively managing teams of 10-20+ people in a physician office to teams with hundreds of people in a hospital setting, I believe the critical steps to building a team that supports your vision and is enjoyable to work with depends upon a few key strategies.

1. **Hire not only for the position but for the individual that will best serve the mission of your company.** I will relate this to a medical weight loss practice. If the position open is one for a physician or other clinician, you want to hire someone with experience in that area. You want to know their educational preparation/credentials along with their clinical experience. For everyone, you want to check references and complete a background check. However, if you are hiring for a medical receptionist, you want someone with experience but if they have the right customer service skills and good office/computer skills, often you can teach them the other specific operational skills.

2. **Understand your team and support their growth.** This is not only helpful for you but important for your team and surprisingly, many find it refreshing since not all leaders take the time to do this.

   At least once a year, you should meet with each staff member if possible to verify what is important to them in their job and inquire about their personal and professional goals. This can be combined with a performance appraisal if necessary. This will help you understand personality issues that may arise and also help you plan for appropriate advancement within the company depending upon their performance. We recently did this and found the following were most important to our medical receptionist and medical assistant staff. These are their direct responses:

- A good reputable physician
- Reliable CRM tool
- Knowledgeable, sales driven staff on program offerings
- Marketing campaign to get them in the door!
- Empathize, acknowledge and LISTEN to determine need – then direct appropriately
- Offer "welcoming support" make patient feel excited to be here; about themselves; and achieving their goals
- Research competition – offer a variety of options (THAT WORK) at varying price points for customer retention – "how we are better and why"
- Proactive, customer service and follow-up
- TEAMWORK…it makes the DREAM WORK!
- Organization
- Ability to multitask
- Compassion – along with this narrative – As a patient walks into a weight loss practice some are already feeling embarrassed, ashamed and even scared of the journey ahead. So compassion is something that everyone working in a weight loss practice should possess. Not only are we

here to help the patient lose weight but we are here to help ease the patient into this life changing journey.

- A well planned friendly and positive environment
- Environment that makes our patients feel safe
- Appropriate accommodations for large patients
- Engaging education and support
- Support (for staff) from physician/management
- Excellent communication

So what do you do with these? It is a great time to review with the physician(s) and management team to discuss if these are being addressed. When obtaining the list from each staff member, that is the time to review what can be improved upon and get their ideas. We expect that if someone comes with a concern or problem, they come with at least on solution for consideration. They rise to the occasion and make the entire process of quality improvement easier and more acceptable to all.

3. **Set clear expectations and communicate regularly.** Your staff wants to do a good job. However, if they are uninformed, they can be put in positions that compromise their ability to do so. Involve them in problem solving and make sure any operational changes are clear to everyone. Discussing any changes together and then following up with a written communication or a copy of the updated operational procedure tends to work well.

4. **Use staff meetings as 30% information and 70% discussion about processes that can be improved upon, new marketing ideas and teambuilding**

exercises. Meetings where you are just receiving information is helpful but in reality, can be quite boring. It almost seems like a dictatorship. Rather, discern what can be communicated via e-mail or other written means and spend your staff meetings to problem solve. I know you might be saying your team is too large or that will create mayhem but in reality, your staff wants to be a part of the solution. So let them.

To make it more controllable, you can set some ground rules so that one person doesn't dominate the discussion. You can set expectations that for anyone who identifies a problem, they need to present at least one solution. You can do team building at the meeting occasionally. All of these things tend to be more productive and contribute to a happier work place.

5. **Consider using employee position contracts that are signed by staff rather than job descriptions.** This improves compliance and an understanding of what the position entails. I recommend including the following areas: Expected Result, Tactical Work Expectations, Position Specific Standards and Companywide Standards (that are the same on all position contracts). If you want to read a great book in which a portion shares how to create position contracts, read *The E-Myth* and/or *The E-Myth Revisited* by Michael Gerber. These are great books for any entrepreneur.

6. **Make sure all staff understands their role as an ambassador for the physician and program.** Your staff members are the primary communicators

with patients. They can be the difference between patients feeling happy or disgruntled, feeling informed or confused. As my office manager recently put it – Patients should immediately feel confident that "We've got this" through specific system(s) that are in place to guide them through their weight loss journey – Start to Finish.

7. **Don't be afraid to discipline an employee who is not compliant with job standards.** You can counsel them and work with them to improve but sometimes you will do yourself (and the employee) a favor if you set them free (according to labor laws and HR policies of course).

8. **Don't tolerate poor customer service.** If you witness an employee demonstrating poor customer service, I recommend addressing it immediately in private. Poor customer service can be contagious and negatively impacts your reputation and your business. Document this behavior in the employee file and continue to monitor the situation. Some people might need additional training and/ or mentoring. Provide such opportunities as appropriate. If the behavior continues, remember that everyone is replaceable. Document and counsel up to and including termination according to your Human Resource policies and standards. It's that important.

9. **Be honest and fair. Enough said!**

10. **Have integrity.** Being moral and ethical is not something you can necessarily teach. I believe integrity is behaving in congruence with what you internally know is right. Integrity is so important

to me and I imagine to you as well. Being able to sleep at night knowing you have done the right thing (even though it might not be the easy thing to do) is a great feeling.

11. **Reinforce that everyone on the team is marketing with each and every interaction.** This expectation needs to be set from the first day on the job. In healthcare, we rarely used to talk about marketing. We just talked about customer service and prompt resolution of complaints. The reality today is that most patients have a choice and while you don't need to treat everyone who walks through your door (some obviously aren't good candidates); you do want to attract ideal candidates you enjoy working with. Everyone needs to understand that with every interaction patients have with your office, you are marketing/promoting what you do. Having this mindset can be the difference between a thriving practice and one that is just getting by.

Your Operations

Your operations refer to all of the processes you must have in place in order to run your program and create an exceptional customer experience. As I mentioned earlier, staff and patients alike crave consistency and order (whether they admit it or not). Having your processes documented helps with new employee orientation and cross training. Cross training is essential, particularly in a smaller program setting.

Operations also helps develop the standards that people are measured against. When a process changes, staff will appreciate knowing that before they have a patient standing in front of them. Remember, you (hopefully) have selected employees that want to do their best. Thus, your job is to provide them with the tools and guidance to do it the best way possible.

Of course at times there is a need for flexibility. But having a basic structure in place will keep your program/practice sane and leave fewer things up to chance.

Your Wow Factor

There has been a lot of discussion about what makes you different, what your 'vibe' is and what your customers want/need. Your Wow factor is what brings your vibe, your operations and your people (staff and patients) together. It is what you do as a leader and as an organization to add uniqueness and enjoyment to what you are doing each and every day. It is being able to take frustrations, figure them out and move forward in a better way. No program or person is perfect but if everyone understands the mission of your organization and the needs of your ideal patients it is easier to try to do the best job they can each and every day.

ABOUT THE AUTHOR

Karol Clark is a best-selling author, speaker and entrepreneur who has a passion for helping physicians integrate effective, profitable weight loss services and retail sales into their practice while improving patient outcomes and enjoying the journey along the way. Her use of non-traditional (easy to implement) medical marketing strategies, along with her dedication to a positive ROI makes her a uniquely different and sought after weight loss business consultant.

Karol is formally trained as masters prepared Registered Nurse in the field of women's health, medical and surgical weight loss, and nutrition. She is also a marketing expert with over 20 years of experience as a hospital administrator, surgical practice administrator, and consultant.

Karol is a certified professional with Author Expert Marketing Machines, Make Market Launch and Publish & Profit. She lives in Virginia with her husband and their four children.

Karol can be reached at
Karol@WeightLossPracticeBuilder.com.

You can also visit her business sites at
www.CFWLS.com, www.WeightLossPracticeBuilder.com,
www.YourBestSellerBook.com and
www.CenterforHormoneHealthandWellness.com.

If you would like a FREE business strategy session,
sign up at www.smarturl.it/bookkarol

REFERENCES

[1] https://obesitymedicine.org/why-is-obesity-a-disease/

[2] https://www.healthline.com/health/obesity-facts#1

[3] https://blog.marketresearch.com/top-6-trends-for-the-weight-loss-market-in-2018

[4] https://obesitymedicine.org/about/about-oma/

[5] https://www.abom.org/

[6] http://scribeamerica.com/blog/physician-reimbursement-why-it-matters-for-the-future-of-american-health-care/

[7] https://en.wikipedia.org/wiki/Concierge_medicine

[8] https://www.stephencovey.com/7habits/7habits-habit2.php

[9] https://www.cms.gov/Outreach-and-Education/Medicare-Learning-Network-MLN/MLNMattersArticles/downloads/MM7641.pdf

[10] https://www.merriam-webster.com/dictionary/accountability

[11] https://www.obesityaction.org/obesity-treatments/what-is-obesity-treatment/medical-weight-management/

[12] https://12weekyear.com/

www.ingramcontent.com/pod-product-compliance
Lightning Source LLC
Chambersburg PA
CBHW060609200326
41521CB00007B/717